DADDY, TEACH US TO PRAY!

PRACTICAL HELP FROM THE PAST FOR FATHERS

Edited by Timothy A. Williams

Daddy, Teach Us to Pray! Practical Help from the Past for Fathers

ISBN (XXXXXXXXXXXXX)

DEDICATION

I dedicate this compiled work to the children and youth of Heritage Baptist Church, which includes my own children. "I have no greater joy than to hear that my children walk in truth." (3 John 4)

TABLE OF CONTENTS

THE LORD'S PRAYER

After this manner therefore pray ye: Our Father which art in heaven, Hallowed be thy name. Thy kingdom come. Thy will be done in earth, as it is in heaven. Give us this day our daily bread. And forgive us our debts, as we forgive our debtors. And lead us not into temptation, but deliver us from evil: For thine is the kingdom, and the power, and the glory, for ever. Amen.

(Matthew 6:9-13)

INTRODUCTION

The Duty of Family Worship

James Fisher defines family worship as "the daily joining of all that are united in a domestic relation, or who are dwelling together in the same house and family, in singing God's praises, Acts 2:47 reading his word, Deut. 6:7, and praying to him, Jer. 10:25." In other words, it is the daily meeting together of a family, in the same room, for a time of worship.

Such worship in the family is a duty daily incumbent upon those who have families. This duty is proven by scriptural precept and example. Yet, we must note that family worship as we know it is not explicitly commanded in the Bible, but the importance of the home in discipleship is prominent throughout the Scriptures.

In the Old Testament, fathers are commanded to teach their children throughout the day, even if that training is informal: "And these words, which I command thee this day, shall be in thine heart: And thou shalt teach them diligently unto thy children, and shalt talk of them when thou sittest in thine house, and when thou walkest by the way, and when thou liest down, and when thou risest up" (Deuteronomy 6:6-7)

However, other passages suggest that this is to be done a more formal basis. For example, in Psalm 78:5-7, we read, "For he established a testimony in Jacob, and appointed a law in Israel, which he commanded our fathers, that they should make them known to their children: That the generation to come might know them, even the children which should be born; who should arise and declare them to their children: That they might set their hope in God, and not forget the works of God, but keep his commandments" (Psalms 78:5-7).

Turning to the New Testament, we find that this Old Testament precedence is continued. Fathers are commanded to bring their children up in discipline and instruction of the Lord (Eph. 6:4). Also, Paul commends the fact that Timothy was trained by his mother and grandmother from childhood in the faith, for which reason he should not easily depart from it (2 Tim. 3:14, 15).

From these Old and New Testament passages, it is clear that the family is central in passing along the faith. And one would have to say, therefore, that family worship is not only warranted, but it is vital.

This obligation for family worship is buttressed by the Scriptural examples which were recorded for our benefit. Some of the examples that we find are Abraham in Gen. 18:19, Joshua in Joshua 24:15, David in 2 Sam. 6:20, Cornelius in Acts 10:2, and especially the example of our blessed Lord, whom we find singing psalms (Matt. 26:30) and praying with his disciples, who were his family (Luke 9:18).

The Importance of Family Worship

Family worship is vital for the planting, watering, and cultivating true saving faith. First, this is done through the very means of instruction. Faith comes by hearing the Word of God. John Bunyan is very pointed on this, when he writes,

> *As touching the spiritual state of his family; he ought to be very diligent and circumspect, doing his utmost endeavour both to increase faith where it is begun, and to begin it where it is not. Wherefore, to this end, he ought diligently and frequently to lay before his household such things of God, out of his word, as are suitable for each particular.*
>
> *Thy children have souls, and they must be begotten of God as well as of thee, or they perish. And know also, that unless thou be very circumspect in thy behavior to and before them, they may perish through thee: the thoughts of which should provoke thee, both to instruct, and also to correct them.*

Family worship is also vital for passing on true faith unto the next generation. George Whitefield saw this as the means of passing on a godly heritage, when he proclaimed, "Would then the present generation have their posterity be true lovers and honorers of God; masters and parents must take Solomon's good advice, and train up and catechize their respective households in the way wherein they should go." Spurgeon echoes those sentiments many years later, when he said,

> *We deeply want a revival of domestic religion. The Christian family was the bulwark of godliness in the days of the puritans, but in these evil times hundreds of families of so-called Christians have no family worship, no restraint upon growing sons, and no wholesome instruction or discipline. How can we hope to see the kingdom of our Lord advance when His own disciples do not teach His gospel to their own children? Oh, Christian men and women, be thorough in what you do and know and teach! Let your families be trained in the fear of God and be yourselves "holiness unto the Lord"; so shall you stand like a rock amid the surging waves of error and ungodliness which rage around us.*

Finally, Family worship is vital because it communicates to our own families and to the world that God is worth worshipping in the home and not merely on Sunday. Putting this in a question form, J. H. Merle D'Aubigne asked, "But, my brethren, if the love of God be in your hearts, and if you feel that, being bought with a price, you ought to glorify God in your bodies and spirits, which are his, where do you love to glorify him rather than in your families and in your houses?" Taking this a little further, Rev. M. Simpson wrote,

> *Family Worship increases the spirit of reverence for God and His Word. Children copy their parents'*

spirit and example. If parents begin the day by invoking God's blessing, by consecrating the early hour to His service, they show their estimate of the value of worship. If business, society, wealth, and pleasure are deferred for worship, the youth feels that the claims of Deity are above all other claims. Parents thus show that they can do nothing rightly without the divine blessing, and that Divine approval is far more precious than the approval of men. God's Book is honored. The Bible is for every day, and for the morning hour of every day. If to the parent it is more precious than gold and sweeter also than the honey and the honey comb, will not the child learn to value a volume so honored and treasured?

It communicates to our own families and to the world that we pursue a real God and not merely a philosophy about God. J. H.Merle D'Aubigne put it like this, as it relates to the teaching of our family,

They are not merely to be taught out of some elementary book that they must love God, but you must show them God is loved. If they observe that no worship is paid to that God of whom they hear, the very best instruction will prove useless; but by means of Family Worship, these young plants will grow "like a tree planted by the rivers of water, that bringeth forth his fruit in his season: his leaf also shall not wither."

The Leader of Family Worship

While parents in general are to be the leaders of family worship, the husband/father is the primary, God-ordained agent to teach his family. As the head of the home, the father is the priest, prophet and king of the home. In this threefold office, the father represents his family before God, represents God to his family, and rules over his family in conformity to God's revealed will.

Part of this leadership is to teach the children to worship the Lord properly. From an historical standpoint, one of the greatest tools used by Christian fathers to teach their children this is a good catechism. Matthew Henry wrote,

> *Oblige them to learn some good catechism by heart, and to keep it in remembrance; and by familiar discourse with them hold them to understand it, as they become capable. It is an excellent method of catechizing, which God Himself directs us to, Deut. vi. 7, to teach our children the things of God, by talking of them as we sit in the house, and go by the way, when we lie down, and when we rise up. It is good to keep up stated times for this service, and be constant to them, as those that know how industrious the enemy is to sow tares while men sleep.*

Yet, the father must lead the family worship. He will teach them more about the worship of God by his actual worship of God than by any other means. He must be a man that is holy and that worships out of the abundance of his own heart's experience. Speaking directly to fathers, Philip Doddridge helpfully remarks,

> *They may learn to conceive aright of the divine perfections, when they hear you daily acknowledging and adoring them: their hearts may be early touched with remorse for sin, when they hear your confessions poured out before God: they will know what mercies they are to ask for themselves, by observing what turn your petitions take: your intercession, may diffuse into their minds a spirit of love to mankind, a concern for the interest of the church and of their country, and what is not, I think, by any means to be neglected, sentiments of loyalty towards our sovereign and his family, when they hear you often invoking the divine blessing upon them: and your solemn thanksgivings for the bounties of Providence, and for benefits of a spiritual nature, may affect their hearts with those gracious impressions towards the gracious Author of all, which may excite in their little breasts love to him, the most noble and genuine principle or all true and acceptable religion: thus they may become Christians by insensible degrees, and grow in the knowledge and love of truth, as they do in stature.*

The Prayer of Family Worship

One of the main parts of the worship of God is prayer. It is incumbent upon families jointly to pray Families ought to pray together because they need to confess mutually affecting sins. Matthew Henry wrote, "How sad is the condition of those families that sin together, and never pray together!" Whitfield Whitefield writes, "[T]here are no families but what have . . . some common sins which they are all to lament and bewail. But how this can be done without joining together in one common act of humiliation, supplication, and thanksgiving is difficult to devise."

Moreover, families must pray to God for their physical and spiritual needs. From whom is it more fitting than a family to pray, "Give us this day our daily bread" (Mt. 6:11)? As families we should jointly ask for physical prosperity; yet, we must also seek the kingdom of God first, asking God to "lead us not into temptation but deliver us from evil." If we are jointly to pray for our daily bread, then how much more ought we to pray for sanctification, the putting off of sin and deliverance from the evil one as a family. Matthew Henry writes,

> *"Praying families are kept from more mischiefs than they themselves are aware of. They are not always sensible of the distinction which a kind providence makes between them and others; though God is pleased sometimes to make it remarkable, as in the story which is credibly related of a certain village in the Canton of Bern in Switzerland, consisting of*

ninety houses, which in the year 1584 were all destroyed by an earthquake, except one house, in which the good man and his family were at that time together praying. That promise is sure to all of the seed of faithful Abraham, 'Fear not, I am thy shield,' Gen. xv. 1. Wisdom herself had passed her word for it, Prov.i. 33. 'Whoso hearkeneth to me,' wherever he dwells, he 'shall dwell safely, and shall be quiet from' all real evil itself, and from the amazing, tormenting fear of evil. Nothing can hurt, nothing needs frighten those whom God protects.

For these reasons, it is incumbent upon the heads of the home to teach their children to pray. It was the normal practice of the Jewish teachers to teach their disciples to pray. John the Baptist taught his disciples to pray after that pattern, and Jesus taught His disciples to pray. Our children will also learn from us. They may learn not to pray; they may even learn to pray wrongly and and thoughtlessly; or we can instruct them by precept and example to pray with biblical content and spiritual affection.

Help for Family Worship

It is obviously best for the father to teach his children systematically, deliberately, and with forethought. It is here that many fathers feel very inept. They do not know feel adequate, which hinders some from beginning. The following material is provided as assistance to the father in teaching his children to pray. It is taken from two main sources:

1. **Rev. James R. Boyd, *The Westminster Shorter Catechism, with Analysis, Scriptural Proofs, Explanatory and Practical Inferences, and Illustrative Anecdotes* (Philadelphia: Presbyterian Board of Publication, 1859). The work has been edited with explanations for the proof texts. These explanations have been provided for the fathers so that they may understand the text of Scripture better. The sources of these explanations were selected from pious writers and with as little technical language as possible. These explanatory notes are within brackets. Also, footnotes have been added to supply the reader with information about certain individuals to whom Rev. Boyd alludes.**

2. **Rev. Dr. Isaac Watts, "To Children and Youth, on the Importance of Prayer," and "Advice relating to Prayer," in *The Publications of the American Tract Society* (New York, American Tract Society, n.d.), Volume 1, Tract 29. These two works by Dr. Watts are added to this work with the hopes that fathers will read them to their children. It may be even hoped that such fathers will find profit for their own souls.**

It is my prayer that that this work may be used by fathers in teaching their children to pray to God. It must be added that the mere perfunctory act of going through this material will never do; the father must have a pious heart affected with a true relationship with God through Christ. May the Spirit of God grant that type of heart to all of us fathers want to train up the next generation of the Church of Christ within our homes for His glory and honor!

CHAPTER ONE: THE NATURE OF PRAYER

Q. 98. What Is Prayer?

Prayer is an offering up of our desires unto God tor things agreeable to his will, in the name of Christ, with confession of our sins, and thankful acknowledgment of his mercies.

What Truths are embraced in this Answer?

1. **Prayer is the offering up of our desires.— Psalm lxii. 8 Pour out your heart before God.**

[English Annotations: "He admonishes us of our wicked nature, who rather hide our sorrows, and bite on the bridle, than to utter our grief to God, to obtain remedy, 1 Sam. i.15"].

[Spurgeon: "Ye to whom his love is revealed, reveal yourselves to him. His heart is set on you, lay bare your hearts to him. Turn the vessel of your soul upside down in his secret presence, and let your inmost thoughts, desires, sorrows, and sins be poured out like water. Hide nothing from him, for you can hide nothing. To the Lord unburden your soul - let him be your only father-confessor, for he only can absolve you when he has heard your confession."]

2. **Prayer must be offered up to the true God.—Isa. xlv. 22, 23. Look unto me, and be ye saved, all the ends of the earth : for I am God, and there is none else.—I have sworn by myself, and the word is gone out of my mouth in righteousness, and shall not return, That unto me every knee shall bow, every tongue shall swear.**

[John Diodati: "'Look' – By faith, conversion, and service, forsaking all manner of idolatry"]

[English Annotations: "He calleth the Gentiles, by the eye of faith, to look after Him, that they may be saved; and not after their idols, which cannot save them, Psa. 34.5; Chapt. 17.7, 8; John 6.40.]

3. **Prayer must be sincere. —Jer. xxix. 13. And ye shall seek me and find me, when ye shall search for me with all your heart.**

[John Calvin: "But God shews that the seasonable time would not come, until their prayers proceeded from a right feeling; this he means by the whole heart. It is indeed certain that men never turn to God with their whole heart, nor is the whole heart ever so much engaged in prayer as it ought to be; but the Prophet sets the whole heart in opposition to a double heart. Perfection, then, is not what is to be understood here, which can never be found in men, but integrity or sincerity."]

4. Prayer must be frequent.—1 Thess. v. 17. Pray without ceasing.

[Adam Clarke: "Ye are dependent on God for every good; without him ye can do nothing; feel that dependence at all times, and ye will always be in the spirit of prayer; and those who feel this spirit will, as frequently as possible, be found in the exercise of prayer."]

[English Annotations: "Be instant and constant in prayer, because we stand in the continual need of God's help, either to give us something good, or to deliver us from something evil. . . ."]

[John Diodati: "This must be understood rather of the heart and affections, than of the tongue and words.]

5. Prayer must be offered up for things only which are agreeable to God's will. — 1 John, v. 14. If we ask anything according to his will, he heareth us.

[John Calvin: "According to his will -- By this expression he meant by the way to remind us what is the right way or rule of praying, even when men subject their own wishes to God. For though God has promised to do whatsoever his people may ask, yet he does not allow them an unbridled liberty to ask whatever may come to their minds; but he has at the same time prescribed to them a law according to which they are to pray. And doubtless nothing is better for us than this restriction; for if it was allowed to every one of us to ask what he pleased, and if God were to indulge us in our

wishes, it would be to provide very badly for us. For what may be expedient we know not; nay, we boil over with corrupt and hurtful desires. But God supplies a twofold remedy, lest we should pray otherwise than according to what his own will has prescribed; for he teaches us by his word what he would have us to ask, and he has also set over us his Spirit as our guide and ruler, to restrain our feelings, so as not to suffer them to wander beyond due bounds. For what or how to pray, we know not, says Paul, but the Spirit helpeth our infirmity, and excites in us unutterable groans. (Rom. 8:26.) We ought also to ask the mouth of the Lord to direct and guide our prayers; for God in his promises has fixed for us, as it has been said, the right way of praying.]

6. **Prayer must be offered up in the name of Christ. — John, xvi. 23. Whatsoever ye shall ask the Father in my name, he will give it you.**

[J. C. Ryle: "In this portion of the verse our Lord renews and repeats His former promise about prayer. 'Until that day when I come again, I solemnly declare that whatsoever things you shall ask in prayer from the Father in my name, He will give them to you'."]

[John Gill: "The medium of access to the Father is the name of Christ; he is the Mediator between God and man, the way of access unto him; whatever is asked, is to be asked on account of his blood, righteousness, and sacrifice, and then there is no doubt of success;

whatever is asked will be given; his blood within the vail speaks loud for every blessing; his righteousness, God is always pleased with; his sacrifice is a sweet smelling savour: his mediation is powerful; and his name is always prevalent."]

7. **Prayer must be offered up with confession of sin. —Dan. ix. 4. I prayed unto the Lord my God, and made my confession.**

[John Calvin: "Here Daniel relates the substance of his prayer. He says, He prayed and confessed before God The greatest part of this prayer is an entreaty that God would pardon his people. Whenever we ask for pardon, the testimony of repentance ought to precede our request. For God announces that he will be propitious and easily entreated when men seriously and heartily repent. (Isa. 58:9.) Thus confession of guilt is one method of obtaining pardon; and for this reason Daniel fills up the greater part of his prayer with the confession of his sinfulness. He reminds us of this, not for the sake of boasting, but to instruct us by his own example to pray as we ought."]

[Albert Barnes: "Not as an individual, or not of his own sins only, but a confession in behalf of the people, and in their name. There is no reason to suppose that what he here says did 'not' express their feelings. They had been long in captivity - far away from their desolate city and temple. They could not but be sensible that these calamities had come upon them on account of their sins;

and they could not but feel that the calamities could not be expected to be removed but by confession of their sins, and by acknowledging the justice of the Divine dealings toward them. When we have been afflicted - when we are called to pass through severe trials - and when, borne down by trial, we go to God, and pray that the evil may be removed, the first thing that is demanded is, that we should confess our sins, and acknowledge the justice of God in the judgments that have come upon us. If we attempt to vindicate and justify ourselves, we can have no hope that the judgment will be averted. Daniel, therefore, in the name of the people, began his prayer with the humble and penitent acknowledgment that all that they had suffered was deserved."]

8. Prayer must be offered up with thanksgiving.—Phil. iv. 6. By prayer and supplication with thanksgiving let your requests be made known unto God.

[Geneva Notes: The third is, that we are not too anxious for anything, but with sure confidence give God thanks, and desire from him whatever we have need of, that with a quiet conscience we may wholly and with all our hearts submit ourselves to him."]

[English Annotations: "So David began very often with tears, but ended with thanksgiving."]

[Adam Clarke: "With thanksgiving, for innumerable favors already received; and for dangers, evils, and deaths turned aside. And let your souls be found in this

exercise, or in the disposition in which this exercise can be performed, at all times, on all occasions, and in all places."]

What Lessons do you derive from the above Doctrines?

I learn (1.) That the words of prayer, however proper and scriptural, do not amount to prayer if they do not express the feelings of my heart. (2.) That it is a great insult to God to address him in the language of prayer, without corresponding desires; in the language of confession, without humility and penitence for the sins confessed; in the language of praise, without an adoring sense of the divine goodness and condescension for the mercies acknowledged. (3.) That I can obtain blessings by prayer only through the mediation and grace of Christ. (4.) That they who do not pray in the method required above, practically deny their dependence on God, their indebtedness to God, their sinfulness and their need of Christ's favor. (5.) That not only private, but family prayer, is a duty and a privilege.

What Illustrations are offered?

1. CAUSE FOB THANKSGIVING.—At a meeting of ministers, as they were inquiring after each other's welfare, one said, " I feel that I have peculiar occasion

for thanksgiving that I am here, for my life was brought into great peril by an accident on the way." "And I," said another, " have surely still greater cause for thanksgiving, seeing that I was brought all the way hither *without any accident at all."*

2. *M'CHEYNE*[1] *ON CONFESSION.*—He says: "I am persuaded that I ought to confess my sins more. I think I ought to confess sin the moment I see it to be sin; whether I am in company, or in study, the soul ought to cast a glance of abhorrence at the sin. If I go on with the duty, bearing the sin unconfessed, I go on with a burdened conscience, and add sin to sin. ***** I ought to confess often the sins of my youth, like David and Paul—my sins before conversion, my sins since conversion—sins against light and knowledge—against love and grace—against each person of the Godhead. I ought to look at my sins in the light of the Holy Law—in the light of God's countenance—in the light of the Cross— in the light of the Judgment-seat—in the light of Hell—in the light of eternity." He further says: "I ought

[1] Robert Murray M'Cheyne (1813-1843) was Scottish minister noted for his piety. He ministered in St. Peter's Church in Dundee until his early death during an epidemic of typhus. After his death, Andrew Bonar published his biography with some of his manuscripts in *The Memoir and Remains of the Rev. Robert Murray M'Cheyne,* which has been used by God in the lives of many. The book is still in being published by Banner of Truth Trust.

to examine my dreams, my floating thoughts—my predilections—my often-recurring actions—my habits of thought, feeling, speech, and action—the slanders of my enemies— and the reproofs and even banterings of my friends—to find out traces of my prevailing sin—matter for confession. I ought to have a number of Scriptures marked, to bring sin to remembrance. I ought, on Sabbath evenings, and on Communion Sabbath evenings, to be especially careful to confess the sins of holy things." —*Memoir,* p. 135.

3. PRAYER OF A ROOMMATE.—The celebrated English preacher and writer, John Angell James,[2] owed his conversion, in the way of means, to the sight of a companion, who slept in the same room with him, bending his knees in prayer on retiring to rest. "That scene, so unostentatious, and yet so unconcealed," says he, "roused my slumbering conscience, and sent an arrow to my heart; for though I had been religiously educated, I had restrained prayer, and cast off the fear of God: my conversion to God followed, and soon afterwards my entrance upon college studies for the work of the ministry."

---

[2] John Angell James (1785-1859) was a noted nonconformist, congregational English preacher of Carrs Lane Independent Chapel in Birmingham. His ministry was a means of the salvation of many, and his works *An Earnest Ministry, The Anxious Inquirer, Christian Progress,* and *Christian Fellowship* have all been recently republished.

4. DR. CHALMERS[3] AND HIS DAUGHER.—The Rev. Dr. Fletcher, of London, having preached with great acceptance to children in Glasgow, Dr. Chalmers invited him to breakfast on the following morning. After breakfast, and family worship, Dr. Chalmers said to him, " Sir, it was not an invitation founded on mere compliment that I gave you last evening to meet me this morning; nor was it to enjoy your conversation. I have a daughter who appears still to have no part or lot with the people of God. If there be any human instrumentality, under God, which can impress her mind, I believe it must be wielded by yourself. I will call her in; and while you are speaking to her, *an agonized father will be speaking to his God.** The result was her hopeful conversion.

5. LUTHER'S PRAYERS. —"No day passes," said a German pastor in 1580, "in which he does not devote at least three hours to prayer and meditation. I once succeeded in hearing him pray. What energy, what faith in his words! He prays earnestly as a man communing

---

[3] Thomas Chalmers (1780-1847), a Scottish Evangelical, came to know the Lord after weighing the credentials of Christianity for an article assigned to him for encyclopedia entry. After the disruption in the Church of Scotland in 1843, Chalmers found himself as the leader of the new Free Church of Scotland. In this post and as the principal the New College, he had a tremendous influence upon many students, such as Robert Murray M'Cheyne, Horatius Bonar, and Andrew Bonar.

with God; and with such trust and faith as a man conversing with his father."

CHAPTER TWO: THE RULE OF DIRECTION IN PRAYER.

Q. 99 What Rule Hath God Given For Our Direction in Prayer?

The whole word of God is of use to direct us in prayer; but the special rule of direction is that form of prayer which Christ taught his disciples, commonly called The Lord's Prayer.

What Truths are embraced in this Answer?

1. **The young and unskillful should be taught to pray. — Luke, xi. 1. Lord, teach us to pray, as John also taught his disciples.**

[Gregory of Nyssa: "He unfolds the teaching of prayer to His disciples, who wisely desire the knowledge of prayer, directing them how they ought to beseech God to hear them."]

[Albert Barnes: We learn, therefore: 1. That the gifts and graces of others should lead us to desire the same. 2. That the true method of praying can be learned only by our being properly taught. Indeed, we cannot pray acceptably at all unless God shall teach us how to pray. 3. That it is proper for us to meditate beforehand what

we are to ask of God, and to arrange our thoughts, that we may not come thoughtlessly into his presence."]

2. We have need to be directed in prayer.—Rom. viii. 26. We know not what we should pray for as we ought.

[John Calvin: "That we are blind in our addresses to God; for though we feel our evils, yet our minds are more disturbed and confused than that they can rightly choose what is meet and expedient. If any one makes this objection — that a rule is prescribed to us in God's word; to this I answer, that our thoughts nevertheless continue oppressed with darkness, until the Spirit guides them by his light."]

[Charles Hodge: "The necessity for this aid arises from our ignorance; we know not what to pray for. We cannot tell what is really best for us. Heathen philosophers gave this as a reason why men ought not to pray! How miserable their condition when compared to ours! Instead of our ignorance putting a seal upon our lips, and leaving our hearts to break, the Spirit gives our desires a language heard and understood of God. As we know not how to pray, the Spirit teacheth us."]

3. The whole word of God is of use to direct us in prayer. —John, xv. 7. If ye abide in me, and my words abide in you, ye shall ask what ye will, and it shall be done unto you.

[J. C. Ryle: "Now, why is there so little power of prayer like this in our own time? Simply because there is so little close communion with Christ, and so little strict conformity to His will. Men do not 'abide in Christ,' and therefore pray in vain. Christ's words do not abide in them, as their standard of practice, and therefore their prayers seem not to be heard. They ask and receive not, because they ask amiss. Let this lesson sink down into our hearts. He that would have answers to his prayers, must carefully remember Christ's directions. We must keep up intimate friendship with the great Advocate in heaven, if our petitions are to prosper.']

[John Gill: "This must be understood not of temporal things, as riches, honours, profits, pleasures, or whatever even the carnal mind of a believer himself may sometimes desire; but of things spiritual, and with such limitations and restrictions as these; whatever is according to the will of God, for the Spirit of God himself asks for no other for the saints; whatever is for the glory of God, and for their own spiritual profit and edification; and whatever is agreeably to the words and doctrines of Christ, which abide in them. Every thing of this kind they ask in faith, and with a submission to the divine will, they may expect to receive."]

[John Calvin: "It is . . . an axiom, that our prayers are faulty, so far as they are not founded on the Word."]

4. **The Lord's Prayer is the special rule given us for our direction in prayer.—**

Mat. vi. 9. After this manner, therefore, pray ye, "Our Father," Etc.

[Geneva Notes: "A true sum and form of all Christian prayers."]

[Martin Luther: "The Lord's Prayer opens with praise and thanksgiving and the acknowledgment of God as a Father; it earnestly presses toward him through filial love and a recognition of fatherly tenderness For supplication, this prayer is unequaled. Hence it is the sublimest and the noblest prayer ever uttered."]

[Matthew Henry: "It is our Lord's prayer, it is of his composing, of his appointing; it is very compendious, yet very comprehensive, in compassion to our infirmities in praying. The matter is choice and necessary, the method instructive, and the expression very concise. It has much in a little, and it is requisite that we acquaint ourselves with the sense and meaning of it, for it is used acceptably no further than it is used with understanding and without vain repetition.

The Lord's Prayer (as indeed every prayer) is a letter sent from earth to heaven. Here is the inscription of the letter, the person to whom it is directed, our Father; the where, in heaven; the contents of it in several errands of request; the close, for thine is the kingdom; the seal, Amen; and if you will, the date too, this day."]

What Lessons do you derive from the above Doctrines?

I learn (1.) The propriety and advantage of using the Lord's Prayer as a daily help in my devotion. (2.) To make myself familiar with all those other parts of the Bible which may both supply me with suitable thoughts and expressions to be used in prayer, and show with what dispositions and aims I am to approach my God in this service. (3.) That I am not required to confine myself to any particular form or forms of prayer. (4.) That having the Bible as a guide and help, all should learn to pray with propriety and acceptance. (5.) Those who do not thus pray, are without excuse.

What Illustrations are given?

1. *MATTHEW HALE,*[4] once Chief-Justice of England, in his Letters to his Children, says: "If I omit praying and reading a portion of God's blessed word in the morning, nothing goes well with me all day."

2. *DR. DODDRIDGE*[5] used often to say, "that he never advanced well in human learning without prayer,

---

[4] Sir Matthew Hale (1609-1676) was famous English jurist who was raised in a Puritan home and accepted this faith until his death. His work as a jurist in English law is unprecedented, strongly influencing the notable William Blackstone.

[5] Philip Doddridge (1702-1751) was an English nonconformist minister, educator, and

and that he always made the greatest progress in his studies when he prayed with the greatest fervency."

3. Towards the close of her last illness, and when able only to speak in short sentences, MRS. *HANNAH MORE*[6] said to a little girl, in whom she was interested: "God bless thee, my dear child; love God; serve God; *love to pray to God more than to do any other thing."*

4. Says PHILIP HENRY:[7] "Let prayer be the *key of the morning,* and the *bolt of the night."*

---

hymn writer. His work *The Rises and Progress of Religion in the Soul* was very influential; it is still in print.

[6] Hannah Moore (1745-1833) was an Evangelical philanthropist, playwright, and writer on religious subjects. She was a fellow abolitionist and friend of William Wilberforce and helped to start twelve schools to teach youth the Bible and the catechism.

[7] Philip Henry (1631-1696) was a nonconformist English minister who was ousted in the notorious Uniformity Act of 1662 and the father of the celebrated commentator Matthew Henry.

CHAPTER THREE: THE PREFACE TO THE LORD'S PRAYER.

Q. 100. What doth Preface of the Lord's Prayer Teach us?

The preface of the Lord's prayer, (which is, " Our Father which art in heaven,") teacheth us to draw near to God with all holy reverence and confidence, as children to a father, able and ready to help us: and that we should pray with and for others.

What Truths are Embraced in this Answer?

1. **We are, in prayer, to approach God with holy reverence. — Psalm. cxlv. 19. He will fulfil the desire of them that fear him: he also will hear their cry, and will save them.**

[Matthew Henry: "The proviso is very reasonable. He will hear and help us, (1.) If we fear him, *if we worship and serve him with a holy awe of him; for otherwise how can we expect that he should accept us?"]*

[John Gill: "That have the true fear of God put into their hearts; that fear him not with a servile, but godly fear; that fear the Lord and his

goodness, and are true worshippers of him in a spiritual and evangelic manner; for the fear of God includes the whole worship of him, private and public: and the Lord grants to such whatever they desire of him, in his fear, under the direction of his spirit, according to his will, and in submission to it."]

2. **We are, in prayer, to approach God with holy confidence.— Eph. iii. 12. In whom we have boldness and access with confidence.**

[John Diodati: This is free access "which is contrary to the terrors of conscience, and to God's rejection."]

[Charles Hodge: "This is the great question which every sinner needs to have answered. — How may I come to God with the assurance of acceptance? The answer given by the apostle and confirmed by the experience of the saints of all ages is, 'By faith in Jesus Christ.' It is because men rely on some other means of access, either bringing some worthless bribe in their hands, or trusting to some other mediator, priestly or saintly, that so many fail who seek to enter God's presence."]

3. **We are, in prayer, to approach God as our Father. — Rom. viii. 15. Ye have received the spirit of**

adoption, whereby we cry, Abba, Father.

[Albert Barnes: "This is an evidence of piety that is easily applied. He that can in sincerity, and with ardent affection apply this term to God, addressing him with a filial spirit as his Father, has the spirit of a Christian. Every child of God has this spirit; and he that has it not is a stranger to piety."]

[Charles Hodge: "That is, 'The Holy Spirit, which you have received, does' not produce a slavish and anxious state of mind, such as those experience who are under the law; but it produces the filial feelings of affection, reverence, and confidence, and enables us, out of the fullness of our hearts, to call God our Father'."]

4. **We are, in prayer, to approach God as being able to help us.—Eph iii. 20. Unto him who is able to do exceeding abundantly above all that we ask or think.**

[John Diodati: "He shows that we cannot ask so much of God by faith, but he will give us much more than we can demand; therefore, we need not fear to be excessive, if we ask in true faith"]

[Charles Hodge: "Paul's prayer had apparently reached a height beyond which neither faith, nor hope, nor even imagination could go, and yet he is not satisfied. An immensity still lay beyond. God was able to do not only what he had asked, but infinitely more than he knew how either to ask or think. Having exhausted all

the forms of prayer, he casts himself on the infinitude of God, in full confidence that he can and will do all that omnipotence itself can effect. His power, not our prayers nor our highest conceptions, is the measure of the apostle's anticipations and desires. This idea he weaves into a doxology, which has in it more of heaven than of earth."]

5. We are, in prayer, to approach God as being willing to help us.— 5. 5. Matt. vii. 11. How much more shall your Father which is in heaven give good things to them that ask him.

[J. C. Ryle: "He illustrates God's readiness to hear our prayers, by an argument drawn from the notorious practice of parents on earth. "Evil" and selfish as they are by nature, they do not neglect the wants of their children according to the flesh. Much more will a God of love and mercy attend to the cries of those who are His children by grace."]

[Matthew Poole: "Asking is but a verbal expression of an inward desire; no man desireth that which is evil, but that which he at least apprehends to be good, that is, suitable unto his wants. As earthly parents, knowing that their children, though through weakness of understanding they may ask that which is really evil for them, yet will not give them any such things, and gratify their ignorance; so neither will your heavenly Father, knowing what you truly need, and what is truly good for

you, give you any thing which he knoweth is not suitable for you, but noxious to you: but if you ask any thing which is either absolutely good for you, and cannot be evil, or which your heavenly Father knoweth to be good for you under your present circumstances, you may be assured, considering he is your Father, and hath as great a kindness for you as an earthly father for his child, and that he is your heavenly Father, and therefore hath a sufficiency to give, will give good things to you asking them of him: and this you may be assured of from that good will and inclination which you, though you come infinitely short of the perfection and good inclinations of your heavenly Father, find in yourselves towards your children; for you derive from him, as his children, all that goodness and benignity which you have. If therefore we in prayer ask any thing of God, which may be good or evil under different circumstances, and receive it not, we may conclude, that though we thought what we asked bread, yet indeed it was a stone; though we thought it a fish, yet God saw it was a scorpion; and account that God answered our general desires, which were for some good, by denying our specific request."]

6. We are to join with others in prayer. — Acts. xii. 12. Many were gathered together, praying.

[Matthew Henry: "They gathered together for prayer on this occasion; though this would made them obnoxious to the government if they were discovered, yet

they know what an encouragement Christ gave to joint-prayer, Matt. 18:19, 20. And it was always the practice of God's praying people to unite their forces in prayer, as 2Chron. 20:4; Esther 4:16"]

[J. C. Ryle: "Let us observe, in the last place, what gracious encouragement Christ holds out to those who meet together in His name. He says, 'Where two or three are gathered together in my name, there am I in the midst of them.' That saying is a striking proof of our Lord's divinity. God alone can be in more places than one at the same time.

There is comfort in these words for all who love to meet together for religious purposes. At every assembly for public worship,—at every gathering for prayer and praise,—at every missionary meeting,—at every Bible reading, the King of kings is present,—Christ Himself attends. We may be often disheartened by the small number who are present on such occasions, compared to those who meet for worldly ends. We may sometimes find it hard to bear the taunts and ridicule of an ill-natured world, which cries like the enemy of old, "What do these feeble people?" (Nehemiah 4:2.) But we have no reason for despondency. We may boldly fall back on these words of Jesus. At all such meetings we have the company of Christ Himself.

There is a solemn rebuke in these words for all who neglect the public worship of God, and never attend meetings for any religious purpose. They turn their backs on the society of the Lord of lords. They miss the opportunity of meeting Christ Himself. It avails nothing to say that the proceedings of religious meetings are marked by weakness and infirmity, or that as much good is got by staying at home as going to church. The words of our Lord should silence such arguments at once. Surely men are not wise when they speak contemptuously of any gathering where Christ is present.

May we all ponder these things. If we have met together with God's people for spiritual purposes in times past, let us persevere, and not be ashamed. If we have hitherto despised such meetings, let us consider our ways, and learn wisdom."]

7. We are to pray for others.— 1 Tim. ii. 1. I exhort therefore, that, first of all, supplications, prayers, intercessions, and giving of thanks be made for all men.

Matthew Henry: "Observe, The design of the Christian religion is to promote prayer; and the disciples of Christ must be praying people. Pray always with all prayer, Eph. 6:18. There must be prayers for ourselves in the first place; this is implied here. We must also pray for all men, for the world of mankind in general, for particular persons who need or desire our prayers. See how far the Christian religion was from being a sect, when it taught men this diffusive charity, to pray, not only for those of their own way, but for all men."]

[John Calvin: "Some might reason thus with themselves: 'Why should we be anxious about the salvation of unbelievers, with whom we have no

connection? Is it not enough, if we, who are brethren, pray mutually for our brethren, and recommend to God the whole of his Church? for we have nothing to do with strangers.' This perverse view Paul meets, and enjoins the Ephesians to include in their prayers all men, and not to limit them to the body of the Church.']

What Lessons do you derive from the above Doctrines?

I learn (1.) That to use this prayer with sincerity, I must be a child of God, and as I am not such by nature, I must be "born again" of the Spirit. (2.) That I should esteem it the greatest privilege to speak to such a Father as this prayer addresses, and to come to him as a child. (3.) Though He is said to be in heaven, yet he also fills immensity, so that he is always near me, and able to help me. (4.) I must learn to confide in my Heavenly Father as able and ready to help his children when they call upon him.

What Illustrations can you give?

1. AN AGED POOR MAN.—One of the members of Christ's flock was reduced to great poverty in his helpless old age, and yet he never murmured. A kind-hearted neighbor who met him on the road, said to him, "You must be badly off. I cannot tell how you maintain yourself and your wife; and yet you are always cheerful." "Oh, not so," replied the old Christian; "we are

not badly off. We have a rich Father, and he does not suffer us to want." "Your father not dead yet! He must be very old indeed." "My Father never dies, and he always takes care of me." That aged Christian was a daily pensioner on the providence of his merciful and covenant-keeping God.

2. A SWEARER. "A child about four years of age would often remark to her mother, with great horror, how Mr G. (a person in the family) swore, and wished to reprove him, but for some time durst not. One day she said to her mother, 'Does Mr. G. say, *Our Father?'* (a term she used to express in her prayers). The mother replied, she could not tell; she then said, 'I will watch, and if he does, I will tell him of swearing so.' She did watch, and heard him say his prayers privately in bed. Soon after this she heard him swear bitterly; upon which she said to him, 'Did you not say *Our Father* this morning?—How dare you swear? Do you think He will be your Father if you swear?' He answered not a word, but seemed amazed; and well he might. He did not live long after this, but was never heard to swear again. 'Out of the mouth of babes and sucklings God has ordained strength'." – from Whitecross' *The Assembly's Shorter Catechism: Illustrated by Appropriate Anecdotes*]

4. CONVERTING THOUGHT: ["A missionary to the heathen writes thus: 'Some impressions of the importance and necessity of true religion, were made upon my mind at a very early period. The first particular one that I recollect, was, I think, when I was about five years of age. There happened one day a very violent

storm of thunder and lightning in our neighbourhood; on which occasion a few Christian friends, who lived near us, terrified by its violence, came into my father's house. When under his roof, in a moment there came a most vivid flash, followed by a dreadful peal of thunder, which much alarmed the whole company, except my father, who, turning toward my mother and our friends, with the greatest composure repeated these lines of Dr Watts—

"The God that rules on high,
And thunders when He please:
That rides upon the stormy sky,
And manages the seas:
This awful God is ours:
Our Father and our love,
He will send down His heavenly powers
To carry us above."

These words, accompanied with such circumstances, sunk deep into my heart. I thought how safe and happy are those who have the great God for their father and friend; but being conscious that I had sinned against Him, I was afraid that He was not my father, and that, instead of loving me, He was angry with me; and this for some time after, continued to distress and grieve my mind.' He then proceeds to say, that these early impressions were succeeded by others, occasioned by parental admonitions, the death of a sister, the conversation of godly friends, and the reading of useful books, which terminated in his conversion." –from Whitecross' *Shorter Catechism Illustrated*"]

CHAPTER FOUR: THE FIRST PETITION IN THE LORD'S PRAYER.

Q. 101. What Do We Pray For in The First Petition?

In the first petition, which is, "Hallowed be thy name;" we pray that God would enable us and others to glorify him in all that whereby he maketh himself known, and that he would dispose all things to his own glory.

What Truths are embraced in is Answer?

1. **Without God we are of ourselves unable to glorify Aim.—2 Cor. iii. 5. Not that we are sufficient of ourselves to think anything as of ourselves; but our sufficiency is of God.**

{John Gill: "Though we are sufficient for this work to which God has called us, and have such trust and confidence that he has blessed and owned us, and done such great things by us; yet we do not ascribe anything to ourselves, to any power of ours, to any self-sufficiency in us: for "we are not sufficient of ourselves" neither for the work of the ministry, nor for the conversion of

sinners, nor for faith and hope in God, nor for any spiritual work whatever; not even to think anything as of ourselves; any good thing, either for our own use and benefit, or for the advantage of others; we are not able of ourselves to meditate with judgment and affection upon the word of God, to study the Scriptures, to collect from them things fit for the ministry; and much less with freedom and boldness to speak of them to edification; and still less able to impress them upon the heart: for though you who are the epistle of Christ are ministered by us, yet not by any power and self-sufficiency of ours."]

[Matthew Henry: "Such are our weakness and inability that we cannot of ourselves think a good thought, much less raise any good thoughts or affections in other men. All our sufficiency is of God; to him therefore are owing all the praise and glory of that good which is done, and from him we must receive grace and strength to do more." This is true concerning ministers and all Christians; the best are no more than what the grace of God makes them. Our hands are not sufficient for us, but our sufficiency is of God; and his grace is sufficient for us, to furnish us for every good word and work."]

2. **We should pray that God would enable us to glorify him. —Psalm li. 15. 0 Lord, open thou my lips, and my mouth shall show forth thy praise.**

[Matthew Poole: "Open thou my lips; which are shut with shame, and grief, and horror. Restore unto me the opportunity, and ability, and liberty which formerly I had of speaking to thee with freedom, and boldness, and familiarity, as this phrase signifies, Ezek. 3:27 24:27 Eph. 6:19,20.']

[John Calvin: This deals with forgiveness of sins, "since it is impossible that we can praise God aright, unless our minds be tranquil and cheerful — unless, as persons reconciled to God, we are animated with the hope of salvation, and 'the peace of God, which passeth all understanding," reign in our hearts' (Phil. 4:7)."]

3. We should pray that God would enable others to glorify him.— Psalm lxvii. 3. Let the people praise thee, O God; Let all the people praise thee.

[Albert Barnes: "Do thou incline them to praise thee: a prayer that all people might so understand the character and ways of God, and might have such a sense of his claims upon them, as to lead them to praise him.']

[Matthew Poole: "O hasten that time, when all the Gentiles shall forsake their dumb idols, and serve and praise thee the living God, as they will have abundant cause to do."]

4. We should pray that God would dispose of all things for the glorifying of himself. — John xii. 28. Father, glorify thy name.

[Matthew Poole: "A general petition, but such a one as all our particular requests must be reduced to, if they be according to the will of God. It is as much as, Father, do thine own will: for God is then glorified when his will is done. But it here signifies more: Not my will, but thy will be done. My flesh indeed saith save me from this hour; but, Father, do thy own will, let that be done concerning me which will most tend to make thy name renowned. Such a prayer never goes without an answer."]

[John Calvin: "By these words he testifies, that he prefers the glory of the Father to all things else, and even neglects and disregards his own life. And the true regulation of all our desires is, to seek the glory of God in such a manner that all other things shall give way to it; for it ought to be reckoned by us an abundant recompense, leading us to endure patiently all that is vexatious or irksome."]

What Lessons do you derive from the above Doctrines?

I learn (1.) That without divine help I cannot entertain sufficiently great, and noble, and devout thoughts of God, nor act with due respect and awe before Him. (2.) The sin of hastily and without some preparation of mind, calling upon God in prayer. (3.) By the "name" of God, I am to understand God himself, by whichever of his names he may be addressed, or thought of. (4.) The great and shocking sin of a profane use or mention of any of the names by which God is made known to us.

What Illustrations can you give?

1. CHILDHOOD'S PRAYER.—A lady, in advanced life, thus writes of herself: "I left home at the age of eleven, alone and unaided, to gain my own livelihood. I went to sea among such as were sailors sixty years ago; and all that prevented me from ruin was the prayer which my mother had taught me nightly. And old as I now am, not a night passes in which I do not offer the Lord's Prayer; scarcely a night without the simple petition of the child—' Now I lay me down to sleep,'" Etc. Such and so powerful were the early teachings of a mother, and such the influence of this prayer.

2. DAVID BRAINERD.8 —Among the dying sayings of this heavenly-minded man, President Edwards has recorded the following: "My heaven is to please God, and to glorify him, and give all to him, and

---

[8] David Brainerd (1718-1747) was an American missionary to the Delaware Indians of New Jersey. His dairy was published by Jonathan Edwards with the hope that many would emulate his godliness. This work highly influenced other important missionaries, such as William Carey, Henry Martyn, and Adoniram Judson.

to be wholly devoted to his glory; that is the heaven I long for; that is my religion; and that is my happiness, and always was, ever since I suppose I had any true religion; and all those that are of that religion shall meet me in heaven. I do not go to heaven to be advanced, but to give honor to God. It is no matter where I shall be stationed in heaven, whether I have a high or a low seat there; but to love, and please, and glorify God is all"

CHAPTER FIVE: THE SECOND PETITION.

Q. 102. What Do We Pray for in the Second Petition?

In the second petition, which is, "Thy kingdom come;" we pray, That Satan's kingdom may be destroyed; and that the kingdom of grace may be advanced, ourselves and others brought into it, and kept in it; and that the kingdom of glory may be hastened.

What Truths are embraced in this Answer?

1. **The kingdom of the universe is God's. — Psal. ciii. 19. His kingdom ruleth over all.**

[Matthew Henry: "But though God's throne is in heaven, and there he keeps his court, and thither we are to direct to him (Our Father who art in heaven), yet his kingdom rules over all. He takes cognizance of all the inhabitants, and all the affairs, of this lower world, and disposes all persons and things according to the counsel of his will, to his own glory (Dan. 4:35): His kingdom rules over all kings and all kingdoms, and from it there is no exempt jurisdiction."]

[John Calvin: The amount is, that whenever God is mentioned, men should learn to ascend in their contemplations above the whole world, because his

majesty transcends the heavens; and they should farther learn not to measure his power by that of man, since it has under its control all kingdoms and dominions."]

2. **Satan has a kingdom in this world. — John xiv. 30. The prince of this world cometh, and hath nothing in me.**

[John Calvin: "The devil is called the prince of this world, not because he has a kingdom separated from God . . . , but because, by God's permission, he exercises his tyranny over the world. Whenever, therefore, we hear this designation applied to the devil, let us be ashamed of our miserable condition; for, whatever may be the pride of men, they are the slaves of the devil, till they are regenerated by the Spirit of Christ; for under the term world is here included the whole human race. There is but one Deliverer who frees and rescues us from this dreadful slavery."]

[J. C. Ryle: "We should note how the devil is called "the prince of this world." He rules and reigns in the hearts of the vast majority of mankind. The whole world 'lieth in the wicked one.' Of the extent and intensity of Satan's influence on earth, even now we have probably very little idea."]

3. **We should pray for the destruction of Satan's authority and kingdom.— Psalm lxviii. 1. Let God arise, let his enemies be scattered: let them also that hate him flee before him.**

[Charles Spurgeon: "We, also, may thus importunately cry unto the Lord, that he would be pleased to make bare his arm, and plead his own cause. "Let his enemies be scattered." Our glorious Captain of the vanguard clears the way readily, however many may seek to obstruct it; he has but to arise, and they flee, he has easily over-thrown his foes in days of yore, and will do so all through the ages to come. Sin, death, and hell know the terror of his arm; their ranks are broken at his approach. Our enemies are his enemies, and in this is our confidence of victory."]

[Geneva Notes: "The prophet shows that even though God permits the wicked tyrants to oppress his Church for a time, yet eventually he will take revenge on them."]

[John Calvin: "There is much comfort to be derived from the circumstance, that those who persecute the Church are here spoken of as God's enemies. When he undertakes our defense, he looks upon the injuries done to us as dishonors cast upon his Divine Majesty. The Psalmist adds a striking figure to illustrate how easily God can overthrow the machinations of our enemies, comparing them to smoke which vanishes when blown upon by the wind, or wax which melts before the fire. We consider it utterly incredible that such a formidable array of opposition should be made to disappear in a moment. But the Spirit takes this method of chiding the fearfulness of our carnal minds, and teaching us that there is no such strength in our enemies as we suppose, — that we allow the smoke of them to blind our eyes, and the solid mass of resistance which they present to

deceive us into a forgetfulness of the truth, that the mountains themselves flow down at the presence of the Lord."]

4. **God has in Christ established a kingdom of grace in the world—Luke i. 33. He shall reign over the house of Jacob for ever; and of his kingdom there shall be no end.**

[Albert Barnes: "He shall reign among his people on earth until the end of time, and be their king forever in heaven. his is the only kingdom that shall never have an end; he the only King that shall never lay aside his diadem and robes, and that shall never die. He is the only King that can defend us from all our enemies, sustain us in death, and reward us in eternity. O how important, then, to have an interest in his kingdom! and how unimportant, compared with 'his' favor, is the favor of all earthly monarchs!"]

[John Gill: "He shall reign in the hearts of his people here unto the end of the world; and with his saints a thousand years in the new heavens and new earth; and with them to all eternity, in the ultimate glory."]

[J. C. Ryle: "Let us beware of spiritualizing away the full meaning of these words. The "house of Jacob" does not mean all Christians. The 'throne of David' does not mean the office of a Saviour to all Gentile believers. The words will yet receive a literal fulfilment, when the Lord Jesus comes the second time, and the Jews are converted. The promise of Gabriel is parallel with

Jer_30:9. The kingdom of which He speaks, is the glorious kingdom foretold in Dan. 7:27, before which all other kingdoms are finally to be overthrown at Christ's second coming."]

5. **We should pray for the advancement of the kingdom of grace. —Isa. lxii. 7. Give him no rest till he establish, and till he make Jerusalem a praise in the earth.**

[John Calvin: "We ought, therefore, to plead with God, and to entreat by earnest prayer, that he will give some success to our labors, which would otherwise be unprofitable. And since we devote ourselves entirely to preaching doctrine, and vigorously oppose all the machinations of Satan, let us learn, at the same time, to turn our minds to God, that he may not permit our labors to be unsuccessful."]

[Albert Barnes: "The idea is, 'Keep not silence yourselves, nor let him rest in silence. Pray without ceasing; and do not intermit your efforts until the desires of your hearts shall be granted, and Zion shall be established, and the world saved'."]

[Keil and Delitzsch: The meaning is that Jehovah's true prophets should "allow Him no rest till He puts Jerusalem in the right state, and so glorifies it, that it shall be recognised and extolled as glorious over all the earth. Prophecy here sees the final glory of the church

as one that gradually unfolds itself, and that not without human instrumentality."]

6. **We should pray that we ourselves be made subjects of Christ's kingdom.—Luke xxiii. 42. Lord, remember me when thou comest into thy kingdom.**

Ness, as quoted by J. C. Ryle: "This short prayer contained a very large and long creed, the articles whereof are these. 1. He believed that the soul died not with the body of man;—2. That there is a world to come for rewarding the pious and penitent, and for punishing the impious and impenitent;—3. That Christ, though now under crucifying and killing tortures, yet had right to a kingdom;—4. That this kingdom was in a better world than the present evil world;—5. That Christ would not keep this kingdom all to himself;—6. That He would bestow a part and portion hereof on those that are truly penitent;—7. That the key of this kingdom did hang at Christ's girdle, though he now hung dying on the cross;—8. That he does roll his whole soul for eternal salvation upon a dying Saviour."

[Jamieson, Fausset, and Brown: "Observe here (1) The 'kingdom' referred to was one beyond the grave; for it is inconceivable that he should have expected Him to come down from the cross to erect any temporal kingdom. (2) This he calls Christ's own (Thy) kingdom. (3) As such, he sees in Christ the absolute right to dispose of that kingdom to whom He pleased. (4) He

does not presume to ask a place in that kingdom, though that is what he means, but with a humility quite affecting, just says, 'Lord, remember me when,' etc. Yet was there mighty faith in that word. If Christ will but "'think upon him' (Neh. 5:19), at that august moment when He "cometh into His kingdom," it will do. 'Only assure me that then Thou wilt not forget such a wretch as I, that once hung by Thy side, and I am content.' Now contrast with this bright act of faith the darkness even of the apostles' minds, who could hardly be got to believe that their Master would die at all, who now were almost despairing of Him, and who when dead had almost buried their hopes in His grave. Consider, too, the man's previous disadvantages and bad life. And then mark how his faith comes out - not in protestations, 'Lord, I cannot doubt, I am firmly persuaded that Thou art Lord of a kingdom, that death cannot disannul Thy title nor impede the assumption of it in due time,' etc. — but as having no shadow of doubt, and rising above it as a question altogether, he just says, 'Lord, remember me when Thou comest,' etc. Was ever faith like this exhibited upon earth? It looks as if the brightest crown had been reserved for the Savior's head at His darkest moment!"]

7. **We should pray that others be brought into the kingdom of grace.—Rom. x. 1. Brethren, my heart's desire and prayer to God for Israel is, that they might be saved.**

[Matthew Henry: "It is our duty truly and earnestly to desire the salvation of our own. This, he says, was his heart's desire and prayer, which intimates, (1.) The strength and sincerity of his desire. It was his heart's desire; it was not a formal compliment, as good wishes are with many from the teeth outward, but a real desire. This it was before it was his prayer. The soul of prayer is the heart's desire. Cold desires do but beg denials; we must even breathe out our souls in every prayer. (2.) The offering up of this desire to God. It was not only his heart's desire, but it was his prayer. There may be desires in the heart, and yet no prayer, unless those desires be presented to God. Wishing and woulding, if that be all, are not praying.]

[John Gill: "This he might desire not only from a natural affection for them, but as a minister of the Gospel, who cannot but wish that all that hear him might be converted and saved; and as a believer in Christ he might pray for this in submission to the will of God; and especially as he knew there was a seed, a remnant according to the election of grace, at that present time among them, that should be saved, though the larger number of them were cast off."]

8. **We should pray that God would keep us in his kingdom of grace.—Psalm. cxix. 117. Hold thou me up, and I shall be safe: and I will have respect unto thy statutes continually.**

[John Gill: "As all are, and none but such, who are in the hands of Christ; enclosed in the arms of everlasting love, upheld with the right hand of Jehovah, supported by his promises and grace, surrounded by his power, sustained by his love, and preserved in Christ Jesus."]

[Geneva Notes: "He desires God's continual assistance, lest he should faint in this race, which he had begun."]

[Charles Spurgeon: "We are saved by past grace, but we are not safe unless we receive present grace. The Psalmist had vowed to keep the Lord's commands, but here he pleads with the Lord to keep him, a very sensible course of procedure."]

9. **We should pray t\at God would keep others in his kingdom of grace.— 1 Thess. v. 23. I pray God your whole spirit, and soul, and body, be preserved blameless unto the coming of our Lord Jesus Christ.**

[Albert Barnes: "It is always proper to pray that God would make his people entirely holy. A prayer for perfect sanctification, however, should not be adduced as a proof that it is in fact attained in the present life.']

[Matthew Henry: "Where the good work of grace is begun, it shall be carried on, be protected and preserved; and all those who are sanctified in Christ Jesus shall be preserved to the coming of our Lord Jesus Christ. And because, if God did not carry on his good

work in the soul, it would miscarry, we should pray to God to perfect his work, and preserve us blameless, free from sin and impurity, till at length we are presented faultless before the throne of his glory with exceeding joy."]

10. There is approaching for the people of God a kingdom of glory.—Rev. xxii. 5. There shall be no night there; and they need no candle, neither light of the sun ; for the Lord God giveth them light: and they shall reign for ever and ever.

[John Gill: True Christians "are made kings now, and in this state they shall reign with Christ for the space of a thousand years; and when they are ended, they shall not cease to reign; nor will Christ, when he delivers up the kingdom to the Father, for his and their kingdom is an everlasting one, Rev. 1:6"]

[Matthew Henry: "The supreme felicity of this paradisiacal state. 1. There the saints shall see the face of God; there they shall enjoy the beatific vision. 2. God will own them, as having his seal and name on their foreheads. 3. They shall reign with him for ever; their service shall be not only freedom but honour and dominion. 4. All this shall be with perfect knowledge and joy. They shall be full of wisdom and comfort, continually walking in the light of the Lord; and this not for a time, but for ever and ever."]

11. We should pray that the kingdom of glory should be hastened.—Rev. xxii. 20. He which testifeth these things saith, Surely I come quietly, Amen. Even so, come, Lord Jesus.

[Matthew Henry: "What comes from heaven in a promise should be sent back to heaven in a prayer, 'Come, Lord Jesus, put an end to this state of sin, sorrow, and temptation; gather thy people out of this present evil world, and take them up to heaven, that state of perfect purity, peace, and joy, and so finish thy great design, and fulfil all that word in which thou hast caused thy people to hope'."]

[Albert Barnes: "That is, as here intended, 'Come in the manner and for the objects referred to in this book.' The language, however, is expressive of the feeling of piety in a more extended sense, and may be used to denote a desire that the Lord Jesus would come in any and every manner; that he would come to impart to us the tokens of his presence; that he would come to bless his truth and to revive his work in the churches; that he would come to convert sinners, and to build up his people in holiness; that he would come to sustain us in affliction, and to defend us in temptation; that he would come to put a period to idolatry, superstition, and error, and to extend the knowledge of his truth in the world; that he would come to set up his kingdom on the earth, and to rule in the hearts of people; that he would come to receive us to his presence, and to gather his redeemed people into his everlasting kingdom. It was appropriate

to the aged John, suffering exile in a lonely island, to pray that the Lord Jesus would speedily come to take him to himself; and there could have been no more suitable close of this marvelous book than the utterance of such a desire. And it is appropriate for us as we finish its contemplation, disclosing so much of the glories of the heavenly world, and the blessedness of the redeemed in their final state, when we think of the earth, with its sorrows, trials, and cares, to respond to the prayer, and to say, "Come, Lord Jesus, come quickly." For that glorious coming of the Son of God, when he shall gather his redeemed people to himself, may all who read these notes be finally prepared. Amen."]

What Lessons do you derive from the above Doctrines?

I learn (1.) To pray that the gospel may be everywhere preached, believed, and obeyed, so that the power of Satan may become less and less in every heart, and that the power of Christ may become greater, and even supreme. (2.) That all men may yield themselves to Christ as their rightful sovereign and Saviour. (3.) That the full effects of the religion of Christ as experienced in heaven are worthy of my earnest desire and prayer.

What Illustrations can you give?

1. REV. DR. GRIFFIN.[9]— In his diary he says: "The three strongest desires which have habitually influenced me for years are: (1.) To be delivered from sin. If this could be, I could bear anything, and be happy in poverty and disgrace. (2.) To enjoy God. I think I surely long more for this than riches or honors, and 'would give up everything for it. (3.) That God's kingdom may come. When I hear of any appearance favorable to Zion, my heart is glad."

2. REV. DR. CHARLES HALL.[10] —He had devoted his children to God. He most earnestly desired to see them all not only Christians, but eminently useful Christians. In a letter to one of his sons, after a vivid sketch of the peculiarities of the age, this passage follows:—" You -will soon come, if your life is spared, upon the stage, right in the *forenoon* of a day of action, such as the world never saw. I would fain impress you

---

[9] Edward Dorr Griffin (1770-1837) was an American was a Congregational minister highly useful in the 2nd Great Awakening. He was a professor of Rhetoric at Andover Theological Seminary (1809-1811) and then president of Williams College (1821-1836).

[10] Charles Hall (1799-1853) was Presbyterian minister, graduate of Hamilton College and studied at Princeton. He was one of the founders of Chi Phi Society and promoted home and foreign missions.

with the idea, that you are to live in an *uncommon era* ; and that you owe it to your own character, to God, and to the interests of human nature, to *be* more, and *do* more, than if you had lived at another time.—*[Dr. Smith's Discourses.]*

3. JONATHAN EDWARDS.[11]—In his account of his views and feelings soon after he received the hope of salvation, President Edwards says: "My heart was knit in affection to those in whom were appearances of piety, and I could bear the thoughts of no other company, but such as were holy, and disciples of the blessed Jesus. I had a great longing for the advancement of Christ's kingdom in the world. My secret prayer used to be in great part taken up in praying for it. If I heard the least hint of anything that happened in any part of the world, that appeared to me in some respect or other, to have a favorable aspect on the interest of Christ's kingdom, my soul eagerly catched at it, and it would much animate and refresh me. I used to be earnest to read public newsletters, mainly for that end; to see if I could find some news favorable to the interest of religion in the world." He regarded (says the *Puritan)* the history of the world as the history of redemption. Every event furnished him with an occasion of thanksgiving or of prayer. — The same was true of the apostolic

[11] Jonathan Edwards (1703-1758) was a Congregational minister who is widely known for his intellectual ingenuity. He played a critical role in the First Great Awakening, experiencing, defending and promoting true revival

ELLIOT.[12] When incidents had been related in his hearing, and had formed the subject of conversation, he used to say, "Now let us turn all this into prayer."

4. A TOO COMMON INCONSISTENCY. — If persons who have money to spare for a thousand superfluities, or even for a thousand mischievous indulgences, do almost nothing for the spiritual welfare of others, what a condemning contrast do they exhibit between their prayers and their conduct! *Either let men live to promote the kingdom of God, or cease to pray that it may come.* If they will live so as to promote the world's sensuality, scepticism, and ungodliness, then let them never more utter the petitions which they do not mean; and if they will not labor for the world's conversion, let them not pretend to pray for it.—*Noel.*

---

[12] John Eliot (1604-1690) was a missionary to the American Indians, often being called "The Indian Apostle." His work in editing the Bay Psalm Book and his translation of the Bible into a native tongue remain outstanding examples of his efforts for the advancement of God's kingdom.

CHAPTER SIX: THE THIRD PETITION.

Q. 103. What Do We Pray For In the Third Petition?

In the third petition, which is, " Thy will be done in earth, as it is in heaven ;" we pray, That God by his grace, would make us able and willing to know, obey, and submit to his will in all things, as the angels do in heaven.

What Truths are embraced in this Answer?

1. **We are of ourselves unable to know or to do the will of God. —1 Cor. ii. 14. The natural man receiveth not the things of the Spirit of God: for they are foolishness unto him: neither can he know them, because they are spiritually discerned.**

[Charles Hodge: "The natural or unrenewed man does not receive the things of the Spirit. As the things which the Holy Ghost has revealed address themselves not only to the intellect as true, but to the conscience as obligatory and to the affections as excellent and lovely, not to receive them, is not to recognize, in our inward experience, their truth, authority, and excellence. . . What, therefore, the apostle here affirms of the

natural or unrenewed man is, that he cannot discern the truth, excellence, or beauty of divine things. He cannot do it. It is not simply that he does not do it; or that he will not do it, but he cannot. We do not say of a clown that he will not discern the truth, excellence, and beauty of a poem. The difficulty is not merely in his will but in his whole inward state. The thing is foolishness to him. So the scriptures do not say of the natural man merely that he will not discern the things of the Spirit, because the difficulty in his case is not in the will alone, but in his whole inward state. He cannot know them . . . That is, because they are discerned through the Spirit. Therefore those who have not the Spirit cannot discern them. If the effect of sin on the human soul is to make it blind to the truth, excellence and beauty of divine things; if, as the apostle asserts, the natural, or unrenewed, man is in such a state that the things of the Spirit are foolishness to him, absurd, insipid and distasteful, then it follows that he can discern them only through the Spirit. His inward state must be changed by the influence of the Spirit before he can apprehend the truth and excellence of the gospel. There must be congeniality between the perceiver and the thing perceived. Only the pure in heart can see God. If our gospel be hid, says the apostle, it is hid to them that are lost. The only hope of the unrenewed, therefore, is in doing as the blind did in the days of Christ. They must go to him for spiritual discernment; and those who go to him he will in no wise cast out."]

2. **God only can make us able and willing to obey and submit to his will.—Phil. ii. 13. It is God which worketh in yon both to will and to do of his good pleasure.**

[Geneva Notes: A most sure and grounded argument against pride, because we have nothing in us praiseworthy, but it comes from the free gift of God, and is outside of us, for we do not have ability or power, so much as to will well (much less to do well), except only by the free mercy of God."]

[John Calvin: "Now, in the calumny brought forward by them against us – that we make men to be like stones, when we teach that they have nothing good, except from pure grace, they act a shameless part. For we acknowledge that we have from nature an inclination, but as it is depraved through the corruption of sin, it begins to be good only when it has been renewed by God. Nor do we say that a man does anything good without willing it, but that it is only when his inclination is regulated by the Spirit of God. Hence, in so far as concerns this department, we see that the entire praise is ascribed to God, and that what sophists teach us is frivolous – that grace is offered to us, and placed, as it were, in the midst of us, that we may embrace it if we choose; for if God did not

work in us efficaciously, he could not be said to produce in us a good inclination."]

3. **We ought to pray that the will of God may be known and obeyed over all the earth. — Psalm lxvii. 2. That thy way may be known upon earth, thy saving health among all nations.**

[Edward Walford: "The petition here offered is, that the Gospel, God's 'way,' might be universally spread; — a prayer that is not yet accomplished, but is in progress towards completion. The mention of nations and peoples, all of them, intimates, that the time which is the object of supplication is the time when God will no longer be the God of the Jews, but of the Gentiles also."]

[Keil and Delitzsch: "The more graciously God attests Himself to the church, the more widely and successfully does the knowledge of this God spread itself forth from the church over the whole earth."]

[Matthew Henry: "Those that have themselves experimentally known the pleasantness of God's ways, and the comforts of his salvation, cannot but desire and pray that they may be known to others, even among all nations. All upon earth are bound to walk in God's way, all need his salvation, and there is in it enough for all; and therefore we should pray that both the one and the other may be made known to all."]

4. **We ought to pray that God would make us able and willing to know his will.—**

Eph. i. 18. The eyes of your understanding being enlightened; that ye may know what is the hope of his calling, and what the riches of the glory of his inheritance in the saints.

[Charles Hodge: "Having prayed that the Ephesians might be enlightened in the knowledge of God and of divine things, the apostle here prays, as the effect of that illumination, that they may have a proper appreciation of the inheritance to which they have attained."]

[Albert Barnes: The meaning here is, that it would be an inestimable privilege to be made fully acquainted with the benefits of the Christian hope, and to be permitted to understand fully what Christians have a right to expect in the world of glory. This is the first thing which the apostle desires they should fully understand."]

5. **We ought to pray that God would make us able and willing to obey his will. — Psal. cxix. 35. Make me to go in the path of thy commandments; for therein do I delight.**

[John Gill: "Lead, guide, direct me in the path, and use me to it; work in me both to will and to do; give both ability and a willing mind to walk therein; by granting fresh supplies of grace, and more spiritual strength; by drawing with the cords of love, and by putting in him the good spirit of grace, to cause to walk in the statutes of

the Lord, and keep his judgments and do them, Ezek. 36:27."]

[John Calvin: "Let it be remembered, that he does not boast of the inherent working of his nature, but sets forth the grace he has received, that God may complete the work he has begun. "Lord, thou hast given me courage, grant me also strength."]

[Matthew Henry: "His plea to enforce this prayer: 'Lord, bring me to, and keep me in, the way of thy commandments, for therein do I delight; and therefore I pray thus earnestly for grace to walk in that way. Thou hast wrought in me this delight in the way of thy commandments; wilt thou not work in me an ability to walk in them, and so crown thy own work?'."]

6. **We ought to pray that God would make us able and willing to submit to his will.— Acts xxi. 14. The will of the Lord be done.**

[Albert Barnes: This is an instance and an evidence of true piety. It was the expression of a wish that whatever God might judge to be necessary for the advancement of his cause might take place, even though it should be attended with many trials."]

[Geneva Notes: "The will of God bridles all affections in those who earnestly seek the glory of God."]

[Matthew Henry: "When we see trouble coming, and particularly that of our ministers' being silenced or

removed from us, it becomes us to say, The will of the Lord be done. God is wise, and knows how to make all work for good, and therefore 'welcome his holy will.' Not only, 'The will of the Lord must be done, and there is no remedy;' but, 'Let the will of the Lord be done, for his will is his wisdom, and he doeth all according to the counsel of it; let him therefore do with us and ours as seemeth good in his eyes.' When a trouble is come, this must allay our griefs, that the will of the Lord is done; when we see it coming, this must silence our fears, that the will of the Lord shall be done, to which we must say, Amen, let it be done."]

7. **We ought to obey the will of God in all things. —Psalm. cxix. 5, 6. O that my ways were directed to keep thy statutes! Then shall I not be ashamed when I have respect unto all thy commandments.**

8. **We ought to submit to the will of God in all things.—1 Sam. iii. 18. It is the Lord, let him do what seemeth him good.**

[Adam Clarke: "There is much of a godly submission, as well as a deep sense of his own unworthiness, found in these words. He also had sinned, so as to be punished with temporal death; but surely there is no evidence that the displeasure of the Lord against him was extended to a future state."]

{John Gill: "Not what seems good to men, or is so in their esteem, but what seems good to the Lord, who knows what is best for his people, and can do nothing

but what is good; all is good he does; there is nothing but goodness in him, and nothing but goodness comes from him; he does good, and nothing else, and even when he afflicts his people; all he does is well done in creation, providence, and grace: and Eli's desire is, that he would fulfil the good pleasure of his will; he appears to be in an excellent temper, not surly and morose, taking it ill that such a message should be sent him by a child; nor was he unaffected with the case of his family, but humbly submitted to the will of God, and acquiesces in it as good, and neither arraigns his justice, nor murmurs at his providences."]

9. **We ought humbly to obey and submit to the will of God as the angels do in heaven.—Job, i. 21. The Lord gave, and the Lord hath taken away; blessed be the name of the Lord.**

[Matthew Poole: "The sense is, I have no cause to quarrel with God, but much cause to bless and praise him that he did give me such blessings, and suffered me to enjoy them more and longer than I deserved; and that he hath vouchsafed to afflict me, which I greatly needed for my soul's good, and which I take as a token of his love and faithfulness to me, and therefore ministering more matter of comfort than grief to me; and that he hath left me the comfort of my wife, and yet is pleased to continue to me the health of my body, and a composed mind, and a heart to submit to his good pleasure; and

that he hath reserved and prepared such a felicity for me, whom no Chaldeans or Sabeans, no men nor devils, can take away from me."]

[Matthew Henry: "He acknowledged the hand of God both in the mercies he had formerly enjoyed and in the afflictions he was now exercised with: The Lord gave, and the Lord has taken away. We must own the divine Providence, [1.] In all our comforts. God gave us our being, made us, and not we ourselves, gave us our wealth; it was not our own ingenuity or industry that enriched us, but God's blessing on our cares and endeavours. He gave us power to get wealth, not only made the creatures for us, but bestowed upon us our share. [2.] In all our crosses. The same that gave hath taken away; and may he not do what he will with his own? See how Job looks above instruments, and keeps his eye upon the first Cause. He does not say, "The Lord gave, and the Sabeans and Chaldeans have taken away; God made me rich, and the devil has made me poor;" but, "He that gave has taken;" and for that reason he is dumb, and has nothing to say, because God did it. He that gave all may take what, and when, and how much he pleases."]

10. We ought cheerfully to obey and submit to the will of God. —Psal. c. 2. Serve the Lord with gladness: come before his presence with singing.

[Matthew Henry: "By holy joy we do really serve God; it is an honour to him to rejoice in him; and we

ought to serve him with holy joy. Gospel-worshippers should be joyful worshippers; if we serve God in uprightness, let us serve him with gladness."]

[Keil and Delitzsch: "Fear and joy do not exclude one another. Fear becomes the exalted Lord, and the holy gravity of His requirements; joy becomes the gracious Lord, and His blessed service. The summons to manifest this joy in a religious, festive manner springs up out of an all-hopeful, world-embracing love, and this love is the spontaneous result of living faith in the promise that all tribes of the earth shall be blessed in the seed of Abraham, and in the prophecies in which this promise is unfolded."]

11. We ought diligently to obey the will of God— Psalm cxix. 37. Quicken thou me in thy way.

[Matthew Poole: "As I desire that I may be dull and dead in afflictions to worldly vanities; so, Lord, make me lively, and vigorous, and fervent in thy work and service."]

[Jamieson, Fausset, and Brown: "Make me with living energy to pursue the way marked out by Thee. Revive me from the death of spiritual helplessness (Psalm 119:17, 25, 40, 50; Psalm 116:3)."]

12. We ought constantly to obey and submit to the will of God—Psalm cxix. 112. I have inclined my heart to perform thy statutes always, even unto the end.

[Albert Barnes: "He meant to do the will of God. He intended to do this constantly; even forever. No man can be a truly pious man who has any disposition, or any purpose, "ever" to turn away from the service of God."]

{Charles Spurgeon: "He was not half inclined to virtue, but heartily inclined to it. His whole heart was bent on practical, persevering godliness. He was resolved to keep the statutes of the Lord with all his heart, throughout all his time, without erring or ending. He made it his end to keep the law unto the end, and that without end. He had by prayer, and meditation, and resolution made his whole being lean towards God's commands; or as we should say in other words - the grace of God had inclined him to incline his heart in a sanctified direction. Many are inclined to preach, but the Psalmist was inclined to practise; many are inclined to perform ceremonies, but he was inclined to perform statutes; many are inclined to obey occasionally, but David would obey alway; and, alas, many are inclined for temporary religion, but this godly man was bound for eternity, he would perform the statutes of his Lord and King even unto the end Lord, send us such a heavenly inclination of heart as this: then shall we show that thou hast quickened and taught us. To this end create in us a clean heart, and daily renew a right spirit within us, for only so shall we incline in the right direction."

What Lessons do you derive from the above Doctrines?

I learn (1.) That it is my duty to study the Scriptures that I may obtain a better knowledge of what God desires me to do, and to be. (2.) To submit to the calamities and privations that are divinely appointed to me, with a cheerful patience, that shall prompt me to say, as Christ said, "Not as I will, but as thou wilt." (3.) To labor to send the Gospel to all men, and to pray for its success, that all men may be in a condition to be prepared to act in proper obedience to the will of God. (4.) There is deplorable need for putting up, daily and earnestly, this third petition of the Lord's prayer, for almost universally men are seen doing their own will in opposition to the will of their heavenly Father.

What Illustrations are given?

1. HOW TO DO GOD'S WILL.—A Sabbath-school teacher, instructing his class in this portion of the Lord's Prayer, said to them: " You have told me, my dear children, *what* is to be done—*the will of God;* and *where* it is to be done—*on earth;* and *how* it is to be done—*as it is done in heaven.* How do you think the angels and happy spirits do the will of God in heaven, as they are to be our pattern?" The first child replied: "They do it *immediately;"* the second, "They do it *diligently;"*the third, "They do it *always;"* the fourth, "They do it *with all their hearts;"* the fifth, "They do it altogether." Here a pause ensued, and no child appeared

to have an answer; but, after some time, a little girl arose and said, "Why, sir, they do it *without asking any questions."*

2. SUBMISSION TO CIRCUMSTANCES.—Dr. Johnson[13] used to say that a habit of looking on the best side of every event is better than a thousand a year. Bishop Hall[14] quaintly remarks: "For every bad there might be a worse; and when a man breaks his leg, let him be thankful it was not his neck."

3. As the late REV. DR. CHARLES HALL was near the end of life, a friend asked him: " Do you really feel that your heavenly Father is about to call you to rest from your labors?" "I do not know," he answered, " for substance, how that may be; nor do I feel solicitous to know. I leave all that, with all my interests, however great or dear, to the disposal of infinite wisdom and goodness." The last Sabbath but one before his death, his daughter read to him the lines:

---

[13] Samuel Johnson (1709-1784) was an English poet, essayist, moralist, literary critic, biographer, editor and lexicographer. He has left a lasting impact upon the English language and literature.

[14] Joseph Hall (1574-1656) was an English Bishop known for his satire, poetry, religious, and moral writings. He opposed Romanism and defended Anglicanism against the separatism of John Robinson.

"My times are in thy hand;
My God I wish them there:
My life, my friends, my soul I leave,
Entirely in thy care."

Having given the closest attention to the end, he then remarked, with emphasis: "I think I can say that."

4. THE WIDOW'S GRIEF.—*Ebenezer Adams,* an eminent member of the Society of Friends, on visiting a lady of rank, whom he found, six months after the death of her husband, on a sofa covered with black cloth, and in all the dignity of woe, approached her with great solemnity, and gently taking her by the hand, thus addressed her: "So, friend, I see then, thou hast not yet forgiven God Almighty." This reproof had so great an effect upon the lady, that she immediately laid aside her violent grief, and again entered on the discharge of the duties of life.

5. THE DYING BOY.—The son of a Baptist minister, in Massachusetts, aged five and a half years, being asked, when near his death, whether he chose to live with his parents and friends here, or die and be with Jesus in heaven, cheerfully answered: " I would rather die, and be *with Jesus in heaven, and WAIT THERE TILL YOU COME."*

6. DR. DODDRIDGE, being found in tears, when just about to embark for Lisbon, in pursuit of health, remarked: "I am weeping, but my tears are those of joy. I can give up my country, my relations, my friends, into the hands of God; and as to myself, I can as well go

to HEAVEN from Lisbon, as from my own study at Northampton."

7. The REV. JOHN NEWTON,[15] in his seventy-fifth year thus writes to Rev. Samuel Pierce: "I am waiting for my dismission. I desire to leave the *how,* and the *when,* and the *where,* to him who does all things well. My prayer is, that while I live I may live to Him; that when the summons shall arrive, I may be found ready; and that if He sees fit to lay me aside, I may be preserved from the weakness which sometimes clouds old age, even of good men ; that I may not disparage my profession or ministry, by impatience, peevishness, or jealousy; but may retire with a good grace, truly thankful that others are coming forward to serve him, I hope, better, when I can serve Him no longer."

8. [DISOBEDIENT SHEEP]. To an afflicted mother, at the grave of her dead child, it was said, "There was once a shepherd, whose tender care was over his flock day and night. One sheep would neither hear his voice nor follow him; so he took up her little lamb in his arms, and then the sheep came after him."

9. DIFFICULTY OF SUBMITTING TO PRESENT CIRCUMSTANCES.— When I am well, I think I could die contentedly: when I am sick, I am impatient to be well again.—*Adam.*

---

[15] John Newton (1725-1807) was an English Anglican minister, who was saved from a former life as a slave-trader. His wise council was sought out by many, and his experimental Christianity is easily detected in his many hymns.

CHAPTER SEVEN: THE FOURTH PETITION.

Q. 104. What Do We Pray For In The Fourth Petition?

In the fourth petition, which is, "Give us this day our daily bread;" we pray, That of God's free gift we may receive a competent portion of the good things of this life, and enjoy his blessing with them.

What Truths are embraced in this Answer?

1. **Temporal good things may be made a subject of prayer.—Gen. xxviii. 20. If God will be with me, and will keep me in this way that I go, and will give me bread to eat, mid raiment to put on.**

[Albert Barnes: It is the grand and solemn expression of the soul's free, full, and perpetual acceptance of the Lord to be its own God. This is the most frank and open utterance of newborn spiritual liberty from the heart of man that has yet appeared in the divine record. "If God will be with me." This is not the condition on which Jacob will accept God in a mercenary spirit. It is merely the echo and the thankful acknowledgment of the divine assurance, "I am with thee," which was given immediately before."]

2. **Every good thing we enjoy is undeserved by us, and is a free gift from God.—Gen. xxxii. 10. I am not worthy of the least of all the mercies, and of all the truth, which thou hast showed unto thy servant.**

[Matthew Henry: "Self-denial and self-abasement well become us in all our addresses to the throne of grace. Christ never commended any of his petitioners so much as him who said, Lord, I am not worthy (Matt. 8:8), and her who said, Truth, Lord, yet the dogs eat of the crumbs which fall from their master's table, Matt. 15:27 . . . . The best and greatest of men are utterly unworthy of the least favour from God, and just be ready to own it upon all occasions. It was the excellent Mr. Herbert's motto, Less than the least of all God's mercies. Those are best prepared for the greatest mercies that see themselves unworthy of the least."]

3. **We are to seek only what may be necessary for the present day and not be over anxious for the future.—Mat. vi. 34. Take therefore no thought for [or, be not over anxious about,] the morrow: for the morrow shall take thought for the things of itself. Sufficient unto the day is the evil thereof.**

[Chrysostom: "Nothing brings so much pain to the spirit as anxiety and cark. That He says, "The morrow

shall be anxious for itself," comes of desire to make more plain what He speaks; to that end employing a prosopopeia of time, after the practice of many in speaking to the rude populace; to impress them the more, He brings in the day itself complaining of its too heavy cares. Has not every day a burden enough of its own, in its own cares? why then do you add to them by laying on those that belong to another day"]

[J. C. Ryle: "We are not to carry cares before they come. We are to attend to to-day's business, and leave to-morrow's anxieties till to-morrow dawns. We may die before to-morrow. We know not what may happen on the morrow. This only we may be assured of, that if to-morrow brings a cross, He who sends it, can and will send grace to bear it.

"In all this passage there is a treasury of golden lessons. Let us seek to use them in our daily life. Let us not only read them, but turn them to practical account. Let us watch and pray against an anxious and over-careful spirit. It deeply concerns our happiness. Half our miseries are caused by fancying things that we think are coming upon us. Half the things that we expect to come upon us, never come at all. Where is our faith? Where is our confidence in our Savior's words? We may well take shame to ourselves, when we read these verses, and then look into our hearts. But this we may be sure of, that David's words are true, "I have been young, and now am old, yet never saw I the righteous forsaken, nor his seed begging bread." (Psalm 37:25)."]

[John Newton: "I compare the troubles which we have to undergo in the course of the year--to a great

bundle of sticks, far too large for us to lift. But God does not require us to carry the whole bundle at once. He mercifully unties the bundle, and gives us first one stick, which we are to carry today; and then another, which we are to carry tomorrow, and so forth. We can easily manage our troubles, if we would only carry the trouble appointed for each day. But the load will be too heavy for us--if we carry yesterday's burden over again today, and then add the burden of tomorrow to the weight, before we are required to bear it."]

4. **We are to ask for such a portion of the good things of life as God, in his wisdom, sees to be best for us. —Prov. xxx. 8. Feed me with food convenient for me.**

[Albert Barnes; "Literally, 'give me for food the bread of my appointed portion.' The prayer foreshadows that which we have been taught by the Divine Wisdom: 'Give us, day by day, our daily bread'."]

5. **We are to seek God's blessing on what we receive, which alone makes temporal good things valuable. —Prov. x. 22. The blessing of the Lord, it maketh rich, and he addeth no sorrow with it.**

[Geneva Notes: "Meaning that all worldly things bring care and sorrow, where as they who feel the blessings of God have none."]

[Matthew Henry: "Worldly wealth is that which most men have their hearts very much upon, but they generally mistake both in the nature of the thing they desire and in the way by which they hope to obtain it; we are therefore told here, 1. What that wealth is which is indeed desirable, not having abundance only, but having it and no sorrow with it, no disquieting care to get and keep it, no vexation of spirit in the enjoyment of it, no tormenting grief for the loss of it, no guilt contracted by the abuse of it - to have it and to have a heart to take the comfort of it, to do good with it and to serve God with joyfulness and gladness of heart in the use of it. 2. Whence this desirable wealth is to be expected, not by making ourselves drudges to the world (Psalm 127:2), but by the blessing of God. It is this that makes rich and adds no sorrow; what comes from the love of God has the grace of God for its companion, to preserve the soul from those turbulent lusts and passions of which, otherwise, the increase of riches if commonly the incentive."]

What Lessons do you derive from the above Doctrines?

I learn (1.) That God is mindful of my wants in this life, as well as those of the life to come. (2.) That for present mercies of each day I owe him my thanks. (3.) That I should look to God for the needful supplies of each day and hour.

"This day be bread and peace my lot;
All else beneath the sun,
Thou knows't if best bestowed or not,
And let thy will be done."

What Illustration can you relate?

1. THE SCANTY MEAL.—A traveler, overtaken in a storm, sought shelter in a dilapidated and lonely dwelling. Before entering, however, he looked through the gaping crevices, and saw a woman seated at a table, on which was placed a coarse and scanty meal. Her hands and eyes were uplifted. Her lips moved; and, as he listened, he heard her say, "All This, And Heaven Too!"

2. HEBDOMADAL[16] DEVOTIONS. —Some never unite in any form of social prayer but on the Sabbath. To suit their hebdomadal devotions this (fourth) petition should have run: " Give us this *week* our *weekly* bread." But as it now is, we have the supplies of the other six days unasked for. We acknowledge our dependence on God for only a seventh portion of our time.—*Dr. Nevins.*

3. ASKING BLESSINGS UPON FOOD.—"I was on one occasion," says George Pritchard, "dining on board an English ship of war, with Queen Pomare,[17] other members of the royal family, and several chiefs. A large table was prepared on the quarter-deck. All being seated,

---

[16] This is an adjective that means weekly.

[17] Pomare IV was the queen of Tahiti from 1827-1877.

the plates were soon abundantly supplied, but not one of the natives attempted to eat. The captain was greatly surprised at this, and said to me: "Mr. Pritchard, I fear we have not provided such food as the natives like: I don't see one of them begin to eat." I replied: "You could not have provided anything that the natives would like better; the reason why they do not commence eating, simply this: they are accustomed always to ask a blessing." Before I could say anything more, the captain, evidently feeling a little confounded, said: "I beg your pardon, Mr. Pritchard; please to say grace." I immediately "said grace," when the natives soon gave proof that they liked the food which had been provided. One of the officers from the end of the table looked at the captain very significantly, and said: "We have got it to-day !" and then addressing himself to me, said: "Mr. Pritchard, you see what a *graceless* set we are." All the gentlemen seemed to feel the rebuke thus unintentionally given. —*The Missionary's Record.*

CHAPTER EIGHT: THE FIFTH PETITION.

Q.105. What Do We Pray for in the Fifth Petition?

In the fifth petition, which is, " And forgive us our debts, as we forgive our debtors ;" we pray, That God, for Christ's sake, would freely pardon all our sins; which we are the rather encouraged to ask because by his grace we are enabled from the heart to forgive others.

What Truths are embraced in this Answer?

1. ***We should pray for the pardon of sin. —Hos.* xiv. 2. "Take away all iniquity, and receive us graciously. — *See also Ps.* li. 1.**

[Matthew Henry: "God's gracious acceptance, and the blessed fruits and tokens of that acceptance, are to be earnestly desired and prayed for by us in our returning to God."]

[John Gill on Psalm 51:1: "David, under a sense of sin, does not run away from God, but applies unto him, and casts himself at his feet, and upon his mercy; which shows the view he had of his miserable condition, and that he saw there was mercy in God, which gave him

hope; and upon his bended knees, and in the exercise of faith, he asks for it."

2. *Pardon of sin is to be expected only through Jesus Christ.—Eph.* i. 7. "In whom we have redemption through his Word, the forgiveness of sins, according to the riches of his grace."

[Charles Hodge: We are not self-redeemed. Christ is our Redeemer."]

[John Calvin: By his death he has restored us to favor with the Father; and therefore we ought always to direct our minds to the blood of Christ, as the means by which we obtain divine grace. After mentioning that, through the blood of Christ, we obtain redemption, he immediately styles it the forgiveness of sins, — to intimate that we are redeemed, because our sins are not imputed to us. Hence it follows, that we obtain by free grace that righteousness by which we are accepted of God, and freed from the chains of the devil and of death."]

[Geneva Notes: "An expounding of the material cause, how we are made acceptable to God in Christ, for it is he alone whose sacrifice by the mercy of God is imputed to us, for the forgiveness of sins."

3. *We must forgive others.—Col.* iii. 13. "Forbearing one

another, and forgiving one another."

[Adam Clarke: "Who required no satisfaction, and sought for nothing in you but the broken, contrite heart, and freely forgave you as soon as you returned to Him. No man should for a moment harbour ill will in his heart to any; but the offended party is not called actually to forgive, till the offender, with sorrow, acknowledges his fault. He should be ready to forgive, and while he is so, he can neither feel hatred nor malice towards the offender; but, as Christ does not forgive us till with penitent hearts we return unto him, acknowledging our offenses, so those who have trespassed against their neighbor are not to expect any act of forgiveness from the person they have injured, till they acknowledge the offense."]

Albert Barnes: "Christ forgave us: (1) Freely - he did not hesitate or delay when we asked him; (2) Entirely - he pardoned all our offences; (3) Forever - he did it so as to remember our sins no more, and to treat us ever onward as if we had not sinned. So we should forgive an offending brother."]

4. ***God alone can enable us, from the heart, to forgive others.— Gal.* v. 22, 23. "The fruit of the Spirit is love, joy, peace, long-suffering, gentleness, goodness, faith, meekness, temperance; against such there is no law."**

[Matthew Henry: "And here we may observe that as sin is called the work of the flesh, *because the flesh, or corrupt nature, is the principle that moves and excites men to it, so grace is said to be* the fruit of the Spirit, *because it wholly proceeds from the Spirit, as the fruit does from the root: and whereas before the apostle had chiefly specified those works of the flesh which were not only hurtful to men themselves but tended to make them so to one another, so here he chiefly takes notice of those fruits of the Spirit which had a tendency to make Christians agreeable one to another, as well as easy to themselves; and this was very suitable to the caution or exhortation he had before given (Gal. 5:13), that they should* not use their liberty as an occasion to the flesh, but by love serve one another."]

5. *Our being enabled to forgive others, encourages us to ask forgiveness for ourselves.— Luke,* xi. 4. " Forgive us our sins; for we also forgive every one that is indebted to us."

[J. C. Ryle: "The justification of every believer no doubt is a finished and perfect work, and one admitting of no degrees, no increase and no diminution. The moment a man believes on Christ, he is as much justified as Paul or John, and cannot be more justified if he lives to the age of Methuselah. But all this is no reason why he should not daily confess his sins, and daily seek fresh

application of Christ's blood to his conscience. In fact, it is the life of faith to do so. The words of our Lord, in another place, are very teaching: 'He that is washed, needeth not save to wash his feet.' (John 13:10) . . . Let it not be forgotten that every unforgiving and implacable man, who uses the Lord's Prayer, is practically praying that his own sin may not be forgiven at all. He is professing a lie."]

6. *Unless we forgive others, we ourselves shall not be forgiven.— Mat.* xviii. 35. "So likewise shall my heavenly Father do also unto you, if ye from your hearts forgive not every one his brother their trespasses."— *See also Matt.* vi. 14, 15.

[Matthew Poole: "That the not doing of this will be an ill evidence to our souls, that God hath not indeed forgiven us, as well as a bar against such forgiveness; and an ill omen, that some punishment from God expects us in this life, to bring us to a temper more conformable to the gospel, and if not, this life, yet in the life which is to come."]

[J. C. Ryle: "It is clear from this parable that one motive for forgiving others, ought to be the recollection that we all need forgiveness at God's hands ourselves. Day after day we are coming short in many things, 'leaving undone what we ought to do, and doing what we ought not to do.' Day after day we require mercy and pardon. Our neighbors' offenses against us are mere

trifles, compared with our offenses against God. Surely it ill becomes poor erring creatures like us, to be extreme in marking what is done amiss by our brethren, or slow to forgive it.

Another motive for forgiving others, ought to be the recollection of the day of judgment, and the standard by which we shall all be tried in that day. There will be no forgiveness in that day for unforgiving people. Such people would be unfit for heaven. They would not be able to value a dwelling-place to which 'mercy' is the only title, and in which 'mercy' is the eternal subject of song. Surely if we mean to stand at the right hand, when Jesus sits on the throne of His glory, we must learn, while we are on earth, to forgive.

Let these truths sink down deeply into our hearts. It is a melancholy fact that there are few Christian duties so little practiced as that of forgiveness. It is sad to see how much bitterness, unmercifulness, spite, hardness, and unkindness there is among men. Yet there are few duties so strongly enforced in the New Testament Scriptures as this duty is, and few the neglect of which so clearly shuts a man out of the kingdom of God.

Would we give proof that we are at peace with God, washed in Christ's blood, born of the Spirit, and made God's children by adoption and grace? Let us remember this passage. Like our Father in heaven, let us be forgiving. Has any man injured us? Let us this day forgive him. As Leighton says, 'We ought to forgive ourselves little, and others much.'

Would we do good to the world? Would we have any influence on others, and make them see the beauty of true religion? Let us remember this passage. Men who care not for doctrines, can understand a forgiving temper.

Would we grow in grace ourselves, and become more holy in all our ways, words, and works? Let us remember this passage.—Nothing so grieves the Holy Spirit, and brings spiritual darkness over the soul, as giving way to a quarrelsome and unforgiving temper. (Eph. 4:30-32)."]

What Lessons do you derive from the above Doctrines?

I learn (1) That ill-will, a spirit of revenge, or even a want of kind regard, towards any of my fellow-men who may have wronged me, will justly stand in the way of my receiving pardon and love from my heavenly Father, and will shut me out of heaven. (2.) Not only the danger but the moral evil of an unkind and unforgiving disposition, which renders one unlike God. (3.) My constant need of divine help, to keep my mind and heart in this undisturbed, meek, loving frame towards all with whom I have to do. (4.) That if I am not inclined to forgive others, I ought to be ashamed to ask God to forgive my greater sins against him. (5.) I should never cease to thank the Redeemer, that he, by offering himself to die in our stead, made full satisfaction to the justice of God for my sins; yet, so far as I am concerned, pardon is a matter of grace. I have done and suffered nothing, to entitle me to claim the remission of punishment as a right.

"Consider this, —
That in the course of justice, none of us
Should see salvation: we do pray for mercy;
And that same prayer doth teach us all to render The deeds of mercy."
"How shalt thou hope for mercy, rendering none?"
—SHAKESPEARE.

What Illustrations are offered?

1. THE LITTLE BLIND BOY. — A little blind boy was asked -what forgiveness is. His beautiful reply was: "It is the odor that flowers breathe when trampled upon."

2. " WHO ARE THE MEEK?" was a question put by a missionary in Jamaica, when questioning some little black boys on *Mat.* v. One of them very pertinently answered: "Those who give soft answers to rough questions."

3. REV. CHARLES SIMEON,[18] says: "To pass by a transgression is more becoming the Gospel than to resent it. "A man strikes me with his sword, and inflicts a wound. Suppose, instead of binding up the wound, I am

[18] Charles Simeon (1759-1836) was an English Anglican minister in Cambridge whose influence upon the Evangelical party within the Church of England and elsewhere was unparalleled in his day.

showing it to everybody; and after it has been bound up, I am taking off the bandage continually, and examining the depth of the wound, and making it to fester, till my limb becomes greatly inflamed, and my general health is materially affected; is there a person in the world who would not call me a fool *t* Now, such a fool is he also, who by dwelling upon little injuries, or insults, or provocations, causes them to agitate and influence his mind. How much better were it to put a bandage over the wound, and never look at it again?"

4. GENERAL OGLETHORPE[19] AND JOHN WESLEY.[20] — In the course of a voyage to America, Mr. Wesley heard Gen. Oglethorpe, with whom he sailed, making a great noise in the cabin, upon which he stepped in to know the cause. The General immediately addressed him, saying: "Mr. Wesley, you must excuse me; I have met with a provocation too great for man to bear. You know the only wine I drink is Cyprus wine, as it agrees with me best of any; I therefore provided myself with several dozens of it, and this villain (the

---

[19] James Edward Oglethorpe (1696-1785) was a general, philanthropist, and founder of the colony of Georgia. He invited men like Wesley and Whitefield to do missionary work among the native Indians.

[20] John Wesley (1703-1791) was a English Anglican minister, evangelist, founder of the Methodist movement, and refiner of Arminianism with focus on justification by faith alone and the new birth.

servant, who was present almost dead with fear) has drank up the whole of it. But I will be revenged on him. I have ordered him to be tied hand and foot, and to be carried to the man-of-war which sails with us. The rascal should have taken care how he used me so, for I never forgive." "Then, sir," said Mr. Wesley, looking calmly at him, "I hope you never sin." The General, confounded at the reproof, threw his keys to the servant, and bade him do better in future. Here, then, is the point. If we would never forgive, we must never sin. The very proneness to sin which we find in ourselves, should be a most powerful incentive to the cultivation of a spirit of forgiveness. — *Rel. Herald.*

CHAPTER NINE: THE SIXTH PETITION

Q.106. What Do We Pray For In The Sixth Petition?

In the sixth petition, which is, " And lead us not into temptation, but deliver us from evil," we pray that God would either keep us from being tenpted to sin, or support and deliver us when we are tempted.

What Truths are embraced in this Answer?

1. **We should pray that God, if consistent with his will, would keep us from being tempted into sin.—Mat. xxvi. 41. "Watch and pray that ye enter not into temptation."— See also 2 Chron. xxxii. 31.**

[John Gill: "Not that they might not be tempted at all; for none of the saints have been, or are without temptations; and they are needful for them; and it is the will of God they should be attended with them; and he has made gracious provisions for their help and relief under them; but that they might not enter into them, throw themselves in the way of temptation, be surprised by them at an unawares, fall into them headlong, be

immersed in them, fall by them, and be overcome with them, so as to forsake Christ, or to deny him."]

[John Calvin: "And let us observe, that the manner of resistance which is here enjoined is, not to draw courage from reliance on our own strength and perseverance, but, on the contrary, from a conviction of our weakness, to ask arms and strength from the Lord. Our watching, therefore, will be of no avail without prayer."]

[J. C. Ryle: "There is a double nature in all believers. Converted, renewed, sanctified as they are, they still carry about with them a mass of indwelling corruption, a body of sin. Paul speaks of this when he says, "I find a law, that, when I would do good, evil is present with me. For I delight in the law of God after the inward man: But I see another law in my members, warring against the law of my mind." (Rom. 7:21-23.) The experience of all true Christians in every age confirms this. They find within two contrary principles, and a continual strife between the two. To these two principles our Lord alludes when He addresses His half-awakened disciples. He calls the one flesh, and the other spirit. He says, 'The spirit is willing, but the flesh is weak.'

"But does our Lord excuse this weakness of His disciples? Be it far from us to think so. Those who draw this conclusion mistake His meaning. He uses that very weakness as an argument for watchfulness and prayer. He teaches us that the very fact that we are encompassed with infirmity, should stir us up continually to '"watch and pray.'

"If we know anything of true religion, let us never forget this lesson. If we desire to walk with God comfortably, and not fall, like David or Peter, let us never forget to watch and pray. Let us live like men on enemy's ground, and be always on our guard. We cannot walk too carefully. We cannot be too jealous over our souls. The world is very ensnaring. The devil is very busy. Let our Lord's words ring in our ears daily like a trumpet. Our spirits may sometimes be very willing. But our flesh is always very weak. Then let us always watch and always pray."]

2. We should pray for support under temptation. — Psalm cxix. 133. "Let not any iniquity have dominion over me."

[John Calvin: "So long, then, as we are left to ourselves, Satan exercises', over us his despotic sway uncontrolled, so that we have not power to rid ourselves of iniquity. The freedom of the godly consists solely in this — that they are governed by the Spirit of God, and thus preserved from succumbing to iniquity, although harassed with hard and painful conflicts."]

[Adam Clarke: "Let me have no governor but God, let the throne of my heart be filled by him, and none other."]

[Charles Spurgeon: We ask to do all that is right, and to fall under the power of nothing that is wrong. God is our sovereign, and we would have every thought

in subjection to his sway. Believers have no choice, darling sins to which they would be willing to bow. They pant for perfect liberty from the power of evil, and being conscious that they cannot obtain it of themselves, they cry unto God for it."]

3. **We should pray for deliverance from temptation. — 2 Cor. xii. 8. " For this thing I besought the Lord thrice that it might depart from me."**

[Matthew Henry: "The apostle prayed earnestly to God for the removal of this sore grievance. Note, Prayer is a salve for every sore, a remedy for every malady; and when we are afflicted with thorns in the flesh we should give ourselves to prayer. Therefore we are sometimes tempted that we may learn to pray."

[Matthew Poole: "For the removal of this affliction, (of what nature soever it was), for the taking of this thorn out of my flesh, I prayed often. It is lawful for us to pray for the removal of bodily evils, though such prayer must be always attended with a due submission to the wisdom and will of God; they being not evils in themselves, but such trials as God intendeth for our good, (as it was here in Paul's case), and which issue in our spiritual advantage."]

What Lessons do you derive from the above Doctrines?

I learn (1.) That I am constantly exposed to sin as well as to suffering, and that on God alone I must rely for grace to feel and act right. (2.) That it is a wicked and a dangerous thing, for any, after uttering this prayer, to put themselves, unless duty calls, in a situation where they know they will he strongly tempted or inclined to violate God's commands. (3.) To withstand temptation, I must impress my heart with a sense of God's presence and holiness; with my obligation to obey him in all things, and even by the greatest effort; with the evil nature of sin, and the misery consequent upon indulging in it; and with the fact that Christ died to induce me to abandon all sin, and to save me from the power of temptation and from the malicious arts of the Tempter.

What Illustrations are given?

1. "Go to dark Gethsemane,
   Ye that feel the Tempter's power,
   Your Redeemer's conflict see,
   Watch with him one little hour;
   Turn not from his griefs away,
   Learn of Jesus Christ to pray."

2. The REV. CHARLES HALL, while in Stratford-upon Avon, writes: "The great enemy has this day sorely buffeted me, so that my joy has been turned unto mourning. I go to my bed looking to Jesus, or

towards him, for Oh, I do not perceive his smiling face. 'Return, O holy Dove return.'"

3. [Dr Pendleton and Lawrence Saunders, meeting together in the beginning of Queen Mary's reign, talked of the persecution which would likely arise; with regard to which Saunders showed much weakness and fear. Pendleton, on the other hand, boasted of his resolution, that he would endure the severest treatment, rather than forsake Jesus Christ, and the truth which he had professed. Yet not long after, the feeble, faint-hearted Saunders, through the goodness of God, sealed the truth with his blood, while proud Pendleton played the apostate, and turned papist." – from Whitecross' *The Assembly's Shorter Catechism: Illustrated by Appropriate Anecdotes*]

4.[One night, John Newton found a notice put up at the church of St Mary Woolnoth upon which he commented a great deal when he came to preach. The notice was to this effect: 'A young man, having come to the possession of a very considerable fortune, desires the prayers of the congregation, that he may be preserved from the snares to which it exposes him.' 'Now, if the man,' said Newton, 'had lost a fortune, the world would not have wondered to have seen him put up a notice; but this man has been better taught'." – from Whitecross' *The Assembly's Shorter Catechism: Illustrated by Appropriate Anecdotes*]

CHAPTER TEN: CONCLUSION OF THE LORD'S PRAYER,

Q. 107. What Is The Conclusion Of The Lord's Prayer?

The conclusion of the Lord's Prayer, which is, "For thine is the kingdom, and the power, and the glory, for ever, Amen," teacheth us to take an encouragement in prayer from God only ; and in our prayers to praise him, ascribing kingdom, power, and glory to him; and in testimony of our desire and assurance to be heard, we say, Amen.

What Truths are embraced in this Answer?

1. ***We should take our encouragement in prayer from God only.—Dan.* ix. 18. "We do not present our supplications before thee for our righteousness, but for thy great mercies."**

[Matthew Henry: "They take their encouragement in prayer from God only, as knowing that his reasons of mercy are fetched from within himself, and therefore from him we must borrow all our pleas for mercy, and so

give honour to him when we are suing for grace and mercy from him."]

Geneva Notes: "Declaring that the godly flee only to God's mercies, and renounce their own works, when they seek for remission of their sins."]

2. ***In our prayers we should join thanksgiving and praise.* — 1 *Chron.* xxix. 10. "David blessed the Lord before all the congregation; and David said, Blessed be thou, Lord God of Israel, our Father, for ever and ever."**

[Jamieson, Fausset, and Brown: "This beautiful thanksgiving prayer was the effusion overflowing with gratitude and delight at seeing the warm and widespread interest that was now taken in forwarding the favorite project of his life. Its piety is displayed in the fervor of devotional feeling - in the ascription of all worldly wealth and greatness to God as the giver, in tracing the general readiness in contributing to the influence of His grace, in praying for the continuance of this happy disposition among the people, and in solemnly and earnestly commending the young king and his kingdom to the care and blessing of God."]

[Matthew Henry: "He adores God, and ascribes glory to him as the God of Israel, blessed for ever and ever. Our Lord's prayer ends with a doxology much like this which David here begins with - for thine is the kingdom, the power, and the glory. This is properly

praising God - with holy awe and reverence, and agreeable affection, acknowledging, (1.) His infinite perfections; not only that he is great, powerful, glorious, etc., but that his is the greatness, power, and glory, that is, he has them in and of himself, 1Chron. 29:11. He is the fountain and centre of every thing that is bright and blessed. All that we can, in our most exalted praises, attribute to him he has an unquestionable title to. His is the greatness; his greatness is immense and incomprehensible; and all others are little, are nothing, in comparison of him. His is the power, and it is almighty and irresistible; power belongs to him, and all the power of all the creatures is derived from him and depends upon him. His is the glory; for his glory is his own end and the end of the whole creation. All the glory we can give him with our hearts, lips, and lives, comes infinitely short of what is his due. His is the victory; he transcends and surpasses all, and is able to conquer and subdue all things to himself; and his victories are incontestable and uncontrollable. And his is the majesty, real and personal; with him is terrible majesty, inexpressible and inconceivable. (2.) His sovereign dominion, as rightful owner and possessor of all: 'All that is in the heaven, and in the earth, is thine, and at thy disposal, by the indisputable right of creation, and as supreme ruler and commander of all: thine is the kingdom, and all kings are thy subjects; for thou art head, and art to be exalted and worshipped as head above all.' (3.) His universal influence and agency. All that are rich and honourable among the children of men have their riches and honours from God. This acknowledgment he would have the princes take notice of and join in, that they might not think they had merited any thing of God by their generosity; for from God they had their riches and honour, and what they had returned to him was but a small part of what they had received from him. Whoever are great among men, it is God's hand that makes them so; and, whatever strength we have, it is God that gives it to us, as the God of Israel our father, 1Chr. 29:10. Psalm 68:35."]

3. ***In our prayers we should ascribe the kingdom or universal dominion to God.* —1 *Chron.* xxix. 11. "All that is in the heaven and the earth is thine; thine is the kingdom, O Lord; and thou art exalted as head above all."**

4. ***In our prayers we should ascribe all power a td glory unto God.*—1 *Chron.* xxix. 11. "Thine, O Lord is the greatness, and the power, and the glory, and the victory, and the majesty."**

5. ***In prayer we should earnestly desire that God would hear us.—Dan.* ix. 19. O Lord, hear; 0 Lord, forgive; O Lord,**

hearken and do; defer not, for thine own sake, O my God."

{John Calvin: "Here vehemence is better expressed, as I have previously observed. For Daniel does not display his eloquence, as hypocrites usually do, but simply teaches by his example the true law and method of prayer. Without doubt, he was impelled by singular zeal for the purpose of drawing others with him. God, therefore, worked in the Prophet by his Spirit, to render him a guide to all the rest, and his prayer as a kind of common form to the whole Church. With this intention, Daniel now relates his own conceptions. He had prayed without any witness, but he now calls together the whole Church, and wishes it to become a witness of his zeal and fervor, and invites all men to follow this prescription, proceeding as it does not from himself but from God."]

[Albert Barnes: "The language in this verse does not require any particular explanation. The repetition - the varied forms of expression - indicate a mind intent on the object; a heart greatly interested; an earnestness that cannot be denied. It is language that is respectful, solemn, devout, but deeply earnest. It is not vain repetition, for its force is not in the "words" employed, but in the manifest fervour, earnestness, and sincerity of spirit which pervade the pleading. It is earnest intercession and supplication that God would hear - that he would forgive, that he would hearken and do, that he would not defer his gracious interposition. The sins of the people; the desolation of the city; the promises of

God; the reproach that the nation was suffering - all these come rushing over the soul, and prompt to the most earnest pleading that perhaps ever proceeded from human lips.

And these things justified that earnest pleading - for the prayer was that of a prophet, a man of God, a man that loved his country, a man that was intent on the promotion of the Divine glory as the supreme object of his life. Such earnest intercession; such confession of sin; such a dwelling on arguments why a prayer should be heard, is at all times acceptable to God; and though it cannot be supposed that the Divine Mind needs to be instructed, or that our arguments will convince God or influence him as arguments do men, yet it is undoubtedly proper to urge them as if they would, for it may be only in this way that our own minds can be brought into a proper state. The great argument which we are to urge why our prayers should be heard is the sacrifice which has been made for sin by the Redeemer, and the fact that he has purchased for us the blessings which we need; but in connection with that it is proper to urge our own sins and necessities; the wants of our friends or our country; our own danger and that of others; the interposition of God in times past in behalf of his people, and his own gracious promises and purposes. If we have the spirit, the faith, the penitence, the earnestness of Daniel, we may be sure that our prayers will be heard as his was."]

6. ***We should pray with a hope and an humble assurance that God***

will hear us.—Heb. **x. 22. "Let us draw near with a true heart, in full assurance of faith."**

[Adam Clarke: "Being fully persuaded that God will accept us for the sake of his Son, and that the sacrificial death of Christ gives us full authority to expect every blessing we need."]

[Geneva Notes: A most grave exhortation, in which he shows how the sacrifice of Christ may be applied to us: that is, by faith which also he describes by the consequence, that is, by sanctification of the Spirit, which causes us to hope in God, and to procure by all means possible one another's salvation, through the love that is in us one towards another."]

7. ***Our prayers should be concluded with an "Amen."—Psalm*** **cvi. 48. "Let all the people say, Amen."**

[John Calvin: But the only way in which we can expect God to lend a favorable ear to the voice of our supplications is, in the spirit of meekness to submit to his corrections, and patiently to bear the cross which he is pleased to lay upon us. It is with great propriety then, that the prophet exhorts the afflicted captives to bless God, even when he was chastising them with considerable severity. It is to the same purpose that it is added, let the people say, Amen; as if he were commanding them all to consent to the praises of God,

though both privately and publicly they were overwhelmed in a sea of troubles."]

[Albert Barnes: "The idea is, Let all the people join in this; let them all express and declare their assent to this: let them all say, "Be it so." The word "Amen" is a word expressing assent - meaning verily, truly, certainly."]

[Heidelberg Catechism, Question 129: "'Amen' signifies, it shall truly and certainly be: for my prayer is more assuredly heard of God, than I feel in my heart that I desire these things of him."

What Lessons do you derive from the above Doctrines?

I learn (1.) That this prayer should be used with confidence, and assurance of hope, since Christ, the infallible Teacher, who best knows what God's will is, and what he may be pleased to grant, has authorized and directed me to use it. (2.) In prayer I am to have reference to the glory of God as the chief end to be attained by prayer, since it is the chief end for which God made me and all other beings and things. (3.) I should entertain large conceptions of the power of God to confer upon me and others all needed good. (4.) I should call to mind the great supremacy of God, his exalted rank as the King of kings, that I may promptly yield him the deepest reverence, and most largely desire that worship and obedience may be rendered to Him by all his creatures.

What Illustration follows?

1. THE JANEWAY FAMILY, of England, is remarkable in the annals of piety, for the fervor of their devotion and joyful and even exulting state of mind in which they passed from the scenes of time into eternity. As illustrative of the subject in hand, the following expressions of feeling are taken from the record of their last hours: The REV. WILLIAM JANEWAY (the father) said to his son : " My heart is full; I can hold no more. I know now whet that sentence means, 'The peace of God which passeth understanding.' I cannot express what glorious discoveries God hath made of himself to me. Oh, help me to bless the Lord!"

His second son, THE REV. JOHN JANEWAY, observed: 'Death has lost its terribleness—it is nothing. I say, death is nothing, through grace, to me. I can as easily die as shut my eyes, or turn my head and sleep I long to be with Christ; I long to die." When Christians came to see him, he would beg of them to spend all the time with him in praise. " O help me to praise God! I have now nothing else to do, from this time to eternity, but to praise and love God. I have what my soul desires upon earth. I want but one thing, and that is, a speedy lift to heaven. 0 praise, praise, praise that infinite boundless love, that hath, to a wonder, looked upon my soul, and has done more for me than thousands of his dear children. Come, help me with praises, all that's little; come help me, 0 ye glorious and mighty angels, who are so well skilled in this heavenly work of praise! Praise him, all ye creatures upon the earth! Praise is now my work, and I shall be engaged in that sweet employment for ever. Let us s.dg a psalm of praise. Come let us lift up our voice in the praise of the Most High: I with you as long as my breath doth last, and when I have none, I shall do it better." A little before he died, in the prayer, or rather in the praises, he was so wrapt up with admiration and joy, that he could scarce forbear shouting for joy. In the conclusion of the duty, with abundance of faith and fervency, he said aloud, "Amen ! Amen!"

The Rev. JAMES JANEWAY (the third son), just before he died, was also in a remarkably happy and devout frame of mind. Though very weak in body, he broke forthwith a loud voice, "Amen ! Hallelujah!" and desired others to join with him; but as they did not immediately do it, he added, “James Janeway is the only singer." Soon he was transported with joy again, and thus gave expression to it: “Millions of praises to the Most High Jehovah! Heaven and earth praise him 1 To mountains and hills praise him! All ye saints bless Him, who hath visited us in our low estate, and redeemed as, by grace, unto himselfl"

2. [A lady, who had just sat down to breakfast, had a strong impression upon her mind that she must instantly carry a loaf of bread to a poor man who lived about half a mile from her house, by the side of a common. Her husband wished her either to postpone taking the loaf of bread till after breakfast, or to send it by her servant; but she chose to take it herself instantly. As she approached the hut, she heard the sound of a human voice. Willing to hear what it was, she stept softly, unperceived, to the door. She now heard the poor man praying, and among

other things he said—'O Lord, help me; Lord, Thou wilt help me; Thy providence cannot fail; and although my wife, self and children, have no bread to eat, and it is now a whole day since we had any, I know Thou wilt supply me, though Thou shouldest again rain down manna from heaven.' The lady could wait no longer; she opened the door. 'Yes,' she replied; 'God has sent you relief. Take this loaf, and be encouraged to cast your care upon Him who careth for you; and when you ever want a loaf of bread, come to my house.' – from *Whitecross' The Assembly's Shorter Catechism: Illustrated by Appropriate Anecdotes.*]

CHATPER ELEVN: THE CHILD'S GUIDE TO PRAYER, BY REV. DR. WATTS

My dear Young Friends —Give me leave to propose to you a few serious considerations, to awaken your desires to seek after God, and to pray to him in your early years.

1. Consider who and what God is. That he is an Almighty Being, who made the heavens, and the earth, and the sea, and all things that are in them; that he is a Spirit, and that he is everywhere present, though you cannot see him; that he knows all things that you do, and that he can do all that you desire of him ; that he is holy, and hates sin, and yet that he is very good and full of mercy, even to his sinful creatures; that he is the greatest, the wisest, and the best of beings. And does he not expect you should love and honor him, who is so great and so good? Is he not your heavenly Father? Did he not make you to love, and serve, and worship him? And how can you pretend to serve and love him, if you never pray to him?

2. Consider who and what you are. Do not your own hearts and consciences tell you that you have done many things amiss, and that you have provoked that God who made you, to be angry with you, and to take away all your comforts? And are you willing to continue under his anger forever? Do you know how terrible is the

anger of God, who can make you miserable in this world and in that which is to come? And is he not very gracious, to call upon such sinners as you are to pray to him? Is it not necessary, therefore, that you should come humbly before him, and fall down on your knees and confess your sins, and entreat him to lay his anger aside, and to love you, notwithstanding all your offences?

3. Consider what are your wants. Do you not daily need food and raiment, that you may not suffer sharp hunger and cold? Do you not want the continuance of health, that you may not pine away with sickness and pain? Can you keep yourselves alive, or can any of your friends keep you from dying? God is the author of all your comforts; on him you depend for daily food and clothing, for health and strength, for recovery from sickness, and preservation from death. It is from God that you must seek all these things, by prayer.

Are you not exposed to dangers every day, and every night? Do you not need the care of God to keep you? to preserve you from mischief, from fires, and from all evils of every kind? And since you deserve nothing at the hand of God, can you suppose he will watch over you, and cover you from all evil, if you never call upon him, nor ask his favor?

Do you not greatly need the forgiveness of your sins? Do not your sins deserve punishment, both here and hereafter? And are you not desirous to be delivered from this punishment? But can you expect God will pardon and deliver you, if you never pray?

And since you cannot do anything to make recompense to the great and holy God for your offences, how speedily should you apply to Jesus Christ, the Son of God, who now dwells in heaven, and who did once make recompense by his death for the sins of men! He is the great Mediator between God and man. How earnestly should you pray, that you may enjoy the benefit of his mediation, and that he may bring you into a state of peace with God! How should you cry to God, that he will forgive you, for the sake of his well-beloved Son! Since you are sensible that you are guilty sinners, you should not be easy one day, without seeking to God for mercy.

Remember, also, that though your sins were pardoned, yet you have a sinful nature in you, ready to offend God continually. Do you not find yourselves ready to commit new sins? Are you not soon ready to be angry, to strike, or call ill names? Are you never ready to grow uneasy and fret, if other children have better things than you? Are you not ready to disobey your parents, or to spend your time in play, when you should be at work, or learning your book? Are you not sometimes inclined to hide your faults by telling a lie? Do not you find yourselves ready to learn evil words, or to wish evil to others, or take something privately that is not allowed you, or to do something that is forbidden? Do you not see, then, how much you need to pray for the grace of God, to keep you from sin daily?

And are not your minds too ignorant of God and heavenly things? Is it not a pleasure to think, that God has promised his own Holy Spirit, to instruct you in the understanding of holy things, as well as to help you in doing your duty? This is a blessed promise, indeed, to poor ignorant and sinful creatures, such as we are. But can you think God will give his grace, or his Holy Spirit, to them who never pray to him? Do you not read in your Bible, "If fathers give good gifts to their children, how much more shall your heavenly Father give the Holy Spirit to them that ask him?" Do not you know, that Jesus Christ is now gone to heaven, to take care of his people when they leave this world? And do you think Jesus Christ will take care of your soul, when it comes like a stranger into that other world, if you have not committed and entrusted it into his hands by prayer?

You must stand before God, the judge of all, when you die ; and are you prepared to stand before God, if you have not obtained a good hope that God loves you 1 There are but two places in the other world—heaven and hell. Heaven for the righteous, who love God and pray to him; and hell for the wicked, who neither pray to him nor love him. And can you hope that God will save you from hell, and receive you to dwell with himself, and with his Son Jesus Christ, if you never pray to him for these blessings?

4. Consider what your mercies are. How kindly has God dealt with you! Has he not given you parents and friends, who by his order provide food and raiment, and everything convenient for you? How many poor children want these comforts, and are exposed to hunger and cold! Have not your parents and friends taken care that you should be taught to read, and learn many things for your good? Do you not know, that it was God who put it into their hearts, and also made them able to do it? How many thousand poor creatures are there in the land, who

know nothing of God, and cannot read a word! Is it not God who has made this happy difference between you and them? And should you not praise him for his goodness? Have you not seen other children blind, or lame, or foolish? Is it not God who has given you your limbs and your senses? Is it not the same good God, that gives you health and peace, night and day ; and are you not bound to thank him for these mercies ? What! Would you live like the brute beasts, who eat and drink and sleep, and take no notice of the great God, from whose hand all blessings come?

5. Consider what relation you stand in to others. Have you not a father and mother that you are bound to honor and love? And would you never pray that God would bestow his best blessings on them, and make them live long to bring you up in his fear? Have you not brothers or sisters, or other friends and relations? And have you no mercies to ask of God for them? Do not your teachers desire that you should pray to God to bless them, that they may the better instruct you? They pray for you, and you should pray for them.

Since, then, dear children, there are such a multitude of reasons that urge you to pray to God, delay no longer, but begin this religious work immediately; and I humbly pray that God would abundantly assist and bless you therein, that you may learn, from your own experience, how sweet and profitable a thing it is to call upon the name of the Lord.

CHAPTER TWELVE: ADVICE RELATING TO PRAYER, BY REV. DR. WATTS

1. Seek out a proper time to retire alone by yourself, morning and evening, at those seasons wherein you have no other necessary business or duty. And here I would persuade myself, that parents, who take due care of the souls of children, would not only admonish and encourage them to seek God in secret, morning and evening, but would point out a proper place for their retirements.

In the morning, I would generally say, the earlier the better. For if you lose the first opportunity, you will often find that you will be utterly hindered from praying, by other things that may happen. Besides, it is best to call upon God early, and begin the day with religion, that you may beg a blessing on yourself, and on all your business that day. Do not begin with the world in the morning, before you have been with God. In the evening, I cannot say the later the better; but rather embrace the first convenient evening hour that offers, lest you be drowsy. However, it is much better to pray late, than not to pray at all. If, at any time, you are hindered in the morning, be sure, if possible, that you be not hindered in the evening too. But the best way is, to keep pretty nearly the same seasons, every day, for your morning and evening retirements, if your circumstances will allow it.

2. Seek a proper and convenient place for your secret retirements. It is no matter what the place, if it be free from disturbance. A bedchamber is generally a proper place for those who have not the conveniency of closets. Be not afraid to go alone, though it may be sometimes in the dark; you are going to meet with God, and he is ever near to them that call upon him. The presence of God is an almighty security against all manner of evils. Nothing can hurt you while God is with you.

3. If you have time, in your secret worship, read a chapter or two, and a psalm, before you pray. For my part, I could wish there were select portions of Scripture chosen out, and printed by themselves, for children to read in private. However, for want of this, I would recommend the book of Genesis, and of Exodus as far as the twentieth chapter, and the book of Proverbs, and the four Gospels, with some practical chapters out of the epistles, and especially the book of Psalms, to be the chief subjects of their reading in secret, in their younger years. The book of Proverbs abounds in useful lessons of prudence, and instructions of piety. The book of Psalms is full of prayers and praises. And let the word not be read in a careless and hasty manner, but with diligent attention, and with an endeavor to remember something of it every day.

4. Leave your business and sports, and all thoughts of them, behind, when you retire for worship. Let your spirit be composed to great seriousness when you begin to pray. The reading of a chapter will help to compose

your thoughts, and fix them more on divine things. Fall down .upon your knees before God in a humble posture, and remember that you are come into the presence of the great God, that you are going to speak to the Majesty of heaven, whom angels worship, and at whose name devils tremble. Take heed, therefore, that you do not trifle with him, nor take his holy name in vain. He sees your heart, he knows all your thoughts, and he observes all your wanderings. And for your encouragement also remember, that he takes kind notice of every sincere desire that rises from your heart.

5. Take heed that you speak not anything to God in prayer, which is not the sincere thought and desire of your own soul. See to it, that your heart agree to the words of your prayer, or else do not utter them before God. "God is a Spirit; and they that worship him, must worship him in spirit and in truth." He hates a hypocrite, who speaks what he does not mean. Speak nothing, therefore, which is not suitable to your present case, and is not the sense of your own heart.

6. Take notice, every day, what good or evil falls out relating to you, and by this means, perhaps, you will often have some particular thing in your mind to mention before God; it may be, some sin to confess, some sorrow to complain of, some blessing to desire, or some mercy to give thanks for. Then be sure to speak it with freedom, in your own language. The great God, who hears the young ravens when they cry, will much more take notice of the voice and language of young children, when they pray to him; and he understands the

meaning of your heart, though your expressions may not be so proper as you could wish.

7. If any person whatsoever takes notice of your retiring daily to pray to God in secret, never be ashamed of it, nor leave off prayer for fear of being seen or known to be religious. If you are ashamed of worshipping God your heavenly Father, in this world, God will be ashamed to own you for one of his children, in the world to come.

8. When several children join together in prayer, take care that nothing be done with rudeness or confusion, but let all decency and gravity be practised. Let not him that speaks begin, till all are come in, and have fallen down on their knees; and let everyone attend to the words spoken, and lift up his heart to God, in all the several sentences; that the prayer of every one may be accepted of God, and that God may delight to answer the united prayers of children, and pour down his blessing on so religious a family.

9. To sum up all, I should add, let all your behavior in the world, both towards God and towards superiors, and towards your fellows, be such as becomes those who profess religion, and pray to God morning and evening. Let a pious care to please God, and a fear of offending him, run through all your speeches and actions. Honor and obey your parents and teachers; love your brothers and sisters; be courteous and kind to all; abstain from all evil words and sinful works; for your prayers will be useless if you continue in willful sins. The prayers of the wicked, who will not repent, are "an abomination to the Lord."

Make it appear that your hearts are sincere and honest in your prayers to God, by endeavoring always to avoid those sins which you have confessed, as well as to practise those duties in which you have prayed God to assist you; and let it be your daily care to obtain all those blessings, as far as in you lies, which you have asked God to bestow upon you. Thus, while prayer and practice go together, you will become Christians indeed, you will be the comfort and joy of your friends in this world, you will always find acceptance with God through the mediation of Jesus Christ, and in the world to come, be made happy to all eternity.

APPENDIX: THE WESTMINSTER ASSEMBLY'S SHORTER CATECHISM ON PRAYER

Q. 98. What is prayer?

A. Prayer is an offering up of our desires unto God [a], for things agreeable to his will [b], in the name of Christ [c], with confession of our sins [d], and thankful acknowledgement of his mercies. [e]

[a]. Ps. 10:17; 62:8; Matt. 7:7-8
[b]. I John 5:14
[c]. John 16:23-24
[d]. Ps. 32:5-6; Dan. 9:4-19; I John 1:9
[e]. Ps. 103:1-5; 136; Phil. 4:6

Q. 99. What rule hath God given for our direction in prayer?

A. The whole Word of God is of use to direct us in prayer [a]; but the special rule of direction is that form of prayer which Christ taught his disciples, commonly called *The Lord's Prayer.* [b]

[a]. I John 5:14

[b]. Matt. 6:9-13

Q. 100. What doth the preface of the Lord's Prayer teach us?

A. The preface of the Lord's Prayer, which is, *Our Father which art in heaven,* teacheth us to draw near to God with all holy reverence [a] and confidence [b], as children to a father [c], able and ready to help us [d]; and that we should pray with and for others [e].

[a]. Ps. 95:6
[b]. Eph. 3:12
[c]. Matt. 7:9-11, cf. Luke 11:11-13; Rom. 8:15
[d]. Eph. 3:20
[e]. Eph. 6:18; I Tim. 2:1-2

Q. 101. What do we pray for in the first petition?

A. In the first petition, which is, *Hallowed be thy name,* we pray, that God would enable us, and others, to glorify him in all that whereby he maketh himself known [a]; and that he would dispose all things to his own glory [b].

[a]. Ps. 67:1-3; 99:3; 100:3-4
[b]. Rom. 11:33-36; Rev. 4:11

Q. 102. What do we pray for in the second petition?

A. In the second petition, which is, *Thy kingdom come,* we pray, that Satan's kingdom may be destroyed [a]; and that the kingdom of grace may be advanced [b], ourselves and others brought into it, and kept in it [c]; and that the kingdom of glory may be hastened [d].

> [a]. Matt. 12:25-28; Rom. 16:20; I John 3:8
> [b]. Ps. 72:8-11; Matt. 24:14; I Cor. 15:24-25
> [c]. Ps. 119:5; Luke 22:32; II Thess. 3:1-5
> [d]. Rev. 22:20

Q. 103. What do we pray for in the third petition?

A. In the third petition, which is, *Thy will be done in earth, as it is in heaven,* we pray, that God, by his grace, would make us able and willing to know, obey, and submit to his will in all things [a], as the angels do in heaven [b].

> [a]. Ps. 19:14; 119; I Thess. 5:23; Heb. 13:20-21

[b]. Ps. 103:20-21; Heb. 1:14

Q. 104. What do we pray for in the fourth petition?

A. In the fourth petition, which is, *Give us this day our daily bread,* we pray that of God's free gift we may receive a competent portion of the good things of this life, and enjoy his blessing with them [a].

[a]. Prov. 30:8-9; Matt. 6:31-34; Phil. 4:11, 19; I Tim. 6:6-8

Q. 105. What do we pray for in the fifth petition?

A. In the fifth petition, which is, *And forgive us our debts, as we forgive our debtors,* we pray that God, for Christ's sake, would freely pardon all our sins [a]; which we are the rather encouraged to ask, because by his grace we are enabled from the heart to forgive others [b].

[a]. Ps. 51:1-2, 7, 9; Dan. 9:17-19; I John 1:7
[b]. Matt. 18:21-35; Eph. 4:32; Col. 3:13

Q. 106. What do we pray for in the sixth petition?

A. In the sixth petition, which is, *And lead us not into temptation, but deliver us from evil,* we pray, that God would either keep us from being tempted to sin [a], or support and deliver us when we are tempted [b].

[a]. Ps. 19:13; Matt. 26:41; John 17:15

[b]. Luke 22:31-32; I Cor. 10:13; II Cor. 12:7-9; Heb. 2:18

Q. 107. What doth the conclusion of the Lord's Prayer teach us?

A. The conclusion of the Lord's Prayer, which is, *For thine is the kingdom, and the power, and the glory, for ever, Amen.* teacheth us to take our encouragement in prayer from God only [a], and in our prayers to praise him, ascribing kingdom, power, and glory to him [b]; and, in testimony of our desire, and assurance to be heard, we say, *Amen.* [c]

[a]. Dan. 9:4, 7-9, 16-19; Luke 18:1, 7-8
[b]. I Chron. 29:10-13; I Tim. 1:17; Rev. 5:11-13
[c]. I Cor. 14:16; Rev. 22:20

LaVergne, TN USA
11 December 2010
208290LV00001B/66/P

LV00051936694